BEING CLUTCH

HOW THE YOUNG ATHLETE CAN CREATE MENTAL TOUGHNESS THROUGH VISUALIZATION

DANIEL BOTOMOGNO

CONTENTS

INTRODUCTION

"If you can imagine it you can achieve it. If you can dream it you can become it."

— *WILLIAM ARTHUR WARD*

Ask five different people to tell you who they think is the most clutch player of all time, and you'll get five different answers. Different athletes, different sports, different great moments in sports–everyone's got a favorite. You've probably got yours.

But one thing everyone can agree on is that clutch athletes are the ones who perform at their best under extreme pressure, at that crucial moment between winning and losing. They come through in difficult situations—a tie game, or a moment where everything seems lost, when fans are already leaving the stadium because they think they know the final score. The players themselves may have even given up and are just counting down the seconds until that final buzzer, siren, or whistle sounds. In comes that clutch player, the one who reaches down deep to find that final burst of energy, or concentration, or whatever skill-based magic they have hidden away—and they succeed. They win the game.

Being clutch is something you want in day-to-day life, not just sports. Think about a time when you had several exams to take, or a paper due (and you waited until the last minute to complete it—as we've all done). You've needed that reserve of clutch to get that paper done and to succeed on those exams. Panicking about them isn't going to help. You need to stay calm and in control, buckling down and going into the room *knowing* you're going to succeed.

Some people just do this naturally, it's true. They're usually the kind of person who is liked by everyone—students and teachers alike. They're probably not the star of the team (though they might be). But you probably can bring them to mind. They're the confident ones. They have friends and make them easily. They aren't afraid to raise their hand when no one else wants to answer a question in class. They don't just walk down the hallway; they parade. They're afraid of nothing. They are clutch.

Do you have to be someone special, like a Ray Allen – shooter of what is arguably the clutchest shot in NBA history–to be clutch (Nacho 2020)? Or is being able to perform under pressure something that *anyone* can do?

The good news is that science says that you can achieve this state of being if you're in the right state of mind (Fan 2019). In fact, they've determined that things that help you succeed under pressure include confidence and feeling like you're in control, even when you're not (Otten n.d.).

What this means is: You can be clutch too.

You may–or may not–know the name, Gregg Popovich. He's been the head coach of the San Antonio Spurs basketball team since 1996. He's considered to be the "winningest coach" of the NBA and possibly the greatest coach in NBA history (Gregg Popovich 2022). When he was interviewed during the 2015 season about the Spurs' cataclysmic 2013 loss to The Heat, he said, "...I wanted to pull the guys back together and appeal to them and challenge them. I wanted to ask them, 'When you are kicked in the gut, how will you respond?'"

It's a good question. When you're in a place where things are tight, when you're "kicked in the gut", will you fail or succeed? A better question is, "How?" And even, "Why?"

Why do you want to be clutch? Presumably, you're a student athlete. You want to win. You know there is a lot you can do to get skilled in your sport. Training camps and training programs, all designed to enable you to transcend the limits of your skills and develop your talent. But there's more to winning than that. You see it on the professional fields all the time. Great players and experts, skilled enough to make big money playing a game. But not all skilled players can claim those clutch moments that populate the highlight reels and remain a part of sports history mystique forever. Sometimes it takes more than skill.

All you need to do is look at the 1980 US Olympic Men's Hockey Team. A little backstory: in order to get the gold (which, of course, they did–or else we wouldn't be using them as an example), they needed to beat the Russian hockey team.

It was no easy feat. The then-Soviets had won the gold in four previous Olympic Games going all the way back to 1964. And that's not all–they had not lost an Olympic hockey game since 1968, to any other team. In 1980, the Soviets had what was considered an unbeatable team. Their player, Slava Fetisov, was quoted as saying it was, "probably the best team ever put together in the Soviet Union. We never thought of losing, never thought it could happen" (Pakarinen 2016).

When they played the American team in an exhibition game prior to the Olympics, they defeated them 10-3. No one was surprised. The Soviet team was made up of professional players, the best the Soviet Union (now Russia) had to offer. And the American players were college players; most of them had played as Golden Gophers for Coach Herb Brooks at the University of Minnesota. They were mostly native Minnesotians, just "local boys" (US Hockey Hall of Fame 2022).

Who could be intimidated by a Gopher? Not the Soviets. They were highly skilled and disciplined, with a rigorous workout schedule. "'They practiced and trained around 1,200 hours a year,' said Alpo Suhonen, former Team Finland head coach and the first NHL head coach from Europe. '...[the Soviets] skated three times a day, perfecting both their individual skills and their teamwork. They had their set five-man units so everybody knew what the others were doing'"

(Pakarinen 2016). Some people even compared them to robots.

So when the Americans faced them on the ice on February 22, 1980, no one expected them to win. However, by this time, they'd shown the rest of the world that, in spite of their amateur status, they were still a force to be reckoned with, and the arena was sold out for their match-up. And by the third period, the game was tied 3-3, so the Americans were at least earning the Soviets' respect, this game.

And then, team captain Mike Eruzione grabbed a loose puck in the Soviet's zone and slipped it past the Soviet goalie, who some considered the best in the world, with a wrist shot to bring the American team ahead. Talk about clutch. No one could believe the miracle win.

Were the Americans any more skilled than the Soviets? Absolutely not. Had they worked harder than the Soviets? Maybe. Or maybe it was just luck? It's hard to say, but the bottom line is, that was a clutch play. Eruzione did what he'd done thousands of times before—hooked a puck and aimed it at the net.

Repetition and practice have a lot to do with it. You have to make every moment count, every pass, every play. But at the same time, each needs to be routine, just something you do. Here's what NBA great, Ray Allen, said after that NBA championship game in 2013: "There's no target. I don't aim. If I'm aiming, that's when I'm missing. The way I look at it is, just get the ball in the air. You do it over and over again, you should never have a target" (Nacho 2020).

But more than that, in both cases, it was the mindset of the athletes and their confidence that they could get the job done. This book will explore that mindset and show you how you, too, can play like a Eruzione or an Allen. We'll explore things like:

- How to translate training and practice into greater performance in real games.
- How to boost your confidence to unleash the full potential of your skills and talents.
- How to eliminate distractions during games to enhance your focus and amplify the benefits of your athletic training.

We'll explore the psychology of sports and the techniques used by professional athletes to overcome these common obstacles, and we'll discuss things like anxiety and how to make it work for you, visualization as a tool for winning, and learning how to be confident by setting goals off the field so you can make them on the field.

In this book, you'll find thought-exercises to try, and information about how your habits and your nutrition can affect your performance, all in one convenient place. Make these ideas your own by putting them into play, writing them down, and using them as often as you can. Even if you take away only one concept discussed in this book, it will be one more piece of the athletic success puzzle that will give you a winning advantage over your opponents.

Ultimately, these techniques can be applied now in high school, in college, and even when you are an adult. Because–being clutch isn't just what you do (one time); being clutch is who you are.

Are you ready to be clutch? Then let's make it happen!

1

TRAINING THE BRAIN

"If you want to perform at the highest level, you have to prepare at the highest level mentally."

— *TOM BRADY*

Being clutch requires training the mind. In this chapter, we explore the mental and psychological side of success in sports.

Have you ever noticed that your skills are great at practice, but they seem to disappear during game time? You're not alone! This happens to many athletes, and it's been found that it's not a problem with their abilities. Instead, it's all in their minds. Fortunately, there's a way to tap into the mind-body connection to improve your performance when it matters the most.

IT'S ALL IN YOUR MIND

Our minds are powerful. Like computers, they load and store information in school and at work, and are constantly interpreting the environment, social interactions, and more. Our minds can create worlds. They are limitless–until we put limitations on them.

Practice Your Practice Mindset

The 2022 Adam Sandler movie, *Hustle*, is about an NBA scout who finds a unicorn (Zagar et al. 2022). A unicorn, if you don't know, means an amazing, undiscovered player who arrives magically out of nowhere but can change the course of game history. In this case, the unicorn is played by real-life Celtic power forward Juancho Hernangomez; he's a player from Spain (in the movie and in real life). Sandler's character, Stanley, finds him playing–and completely dominating!-- in a street game and talks him into coming to America to sign with the Philadelphia 76ers.

Of course, things happen (or else there wouldn't be a story). During tryouts, another player sizes up "Bo" and decides to get into his head to affect his performance, destroying his chances. So Stanley trains Bo by pushing him through grueling practices and exercises, all while saying the worst things he can think of to distract him. And when it came to the final tryout, he mutters to Bo before the player hits the floor, "Remember, it's just another workout. You've done it a thousand times." Because I don't want to ruin the movie for you, I won't tell you anymore except to say it is a perfect illustration of how your state of mind can affect your performance.

Your state of mind is so important that experts say that not training your mind as you train your body can cost you excellence at game time. Like your muscles, your mind needs the same training, routine, and, especially, discipline to become a part of your skill-set. And it's true–the best athletes know that what you think and how you think at clutch moments is what makes the difference between winning and losing (Luow n.d.). They train their brains just as hard as they train their bodies. Just look at the quote at the beginning of this chapter!

Experts say that athletes commonly have a "practice mindset" and a "performance mindset." This is something Stanley knew as he trained Bo in *Hustle*, and it's why he reminded his player that even though they were at a moment when winning was essential, he needed to work just like he had during practice.

When you practice, you have unlimited and unpressured opportunities to make the shot or get the ball over the line or puck into the net; obviously, the outcome doesn't matter the way it does during game time. So you're relaxed and focused on what you're doing, which is perfecting your skills. If you think about it (which is kind of ironic, but work with me here), you're probably *not* thinking about what you're doing during practice at all (Shintani 2021). Instead, you're just reacting automatically and going through routines and motions and working on your "muscle memory."

Muscle memory, if you don't already know, is the way you do something without conscious thought–like riding a bike or driving a car (among other things). You're in the moment and not looking to the future.

During a game, however, your focus changes. You're no longer in the moment–you're thinking ahead, about how you and your team are going to win, or how well you are performing. It's understandable. The conditions are different. The person you may have a crush on could be sitting in the stands watching you. There could be a college coach or scout watching. In fact, the entire *school* could have their eyes on you! If you make a mistake or miss a shot, *everyone* will know, and you could go down in school history as the worst player anyone has ever seen.

That's kind of terrifying; if it's the type of thought that goes through your head during a game, it will paralyze you. And rest assured, I'm only putting that thought in your head because I'm going to tell you how to get it out of there!

Anyway, once you begin thinking this way, you lose your confidence. In fact, you begin *overthinking*, which turns your focus from the game inward, completely destroying your performance (Shintani 2021). You begin to play cautiously; because you want to avoid making mistakes, you start relying on your thoughts and analysis of what's going on instead of relying on your muscle memory to just react to the situation.

Practice Performing

To avoid performance paralysis, you need to practice playing under pressure (Mark 2018). In fact, this is just as if not more important than developing your skills.

One way to do this is to learn how to switch from practice to performance mindset on demand. Imagine those fans watching you. Better, imagine the non-fans, the ones who may be critical of you. If you drop the ball or trip or miss the cutoff man or whatever it is that's a mistake in your sport, imagine them booing you. Soak it up. And realize–you're okay. You survived. Then pick yourself up and keep going.

This is a good place to tell you that one reason people love sports so much is because they're a reflection of life. Sometimes we succeed, but more often, we fail. The difference between being a mediocre athlete and a great athlete is how you manage to move from failure (or disaster) to success. Learn how to fail first–and then (and more importantly) how to move on to success. This is a skill that will serve you not only during the game but in life, too.

The reason for this is because human beings are not only analytical, they're also emotional. Emotions can cause greater obstacles for us than physical conditions. So learning how to deal with your emotions as you play can make a big difference in your performance. When you give in to sadness or embarrassment or whatever negative emotion you have, you start to think of yourself as a victim. You think, "I could have made that play, but they–" (the fans, the other players, your teammates, etc.)-- "made me feel bad."

When you start thinking this way, you're no longer in the present moment and no longer on the field. Instead, you're thinking about how you don't like the conditions under which you're playing, and not about the game at all (Mark 2018). You might as well be on the bench, sulking and whining (yes, I'm going to use that word and you should too) about how unfair everything is.

Whether you like it or not, people will have opinions and reactions. You can't worry about them. One way to overcome this is by deliberately envisioning or even creating challenging conditions for yourself during your practice sessions. Your goal is not to get good at dealing with these situations, but to accept them without getting emotional and upset, but to continue to focus on the game. In order to combat this, you need to get out of your head and back into your game. But how?

Get Out of Your Head and Back in the Game

I like the way the character named Benny put it in what has been called one of the best baseball movies of all time, *The Sandlot* (David Mickey Evans and Gunter 1993): *"*Man, this is baseball. You gotta stop thinking. Just have fun. I mean, if you were having fun you would've caught that ball." You can't put it any better than that, so...

- **"Just have fun."** Don't try to control everything. You can't. Don't worry about being perfect. You won't be. All you need to think about (if anything) is having fun. Enjoy what you're doing–otherwise, why bother even playing?

There's a reason they say you're "playing" a game. Go. Play. Have fun, just like you do in practice. And then, during the game...

- **Tell yourself, "it's just like practice."** Of course, this is easier to say than to do, but try to focus on what you're doing in the moment. There are a thousand quotes about this very thing. One of them is: "football is a game of inches, and inches make the champion," which means you need to focus on each play and move the ball or puck to the paint or end zone one play at a time, one inch at a time.

- **And then, *play* like it's practice.** If you play like you do during practice, without worrying about the fans in the stands or the ultimate outcome, you'll trick yourself (kind of) out of your head and into your skills. In a way, you need to practice playing like you're practicing. (Which sounds weird, but makes sense if you think about it.) It takes effort to learn to do this, but once you do, you'll be unstoppable.

- **There is no "big picture."** By this, I mean, don't worry about the outcome of the game. Don't worry about your performance. In fact, don't have any expectations of how you "should" play. Just play. The Nike brand's slogan sums it up perfectly: *"Just do it."*

- **Stop thinking!** You can't think yourself into a great play. Trust your body to do the job. You've repeated countless variations of whatever you need to do during practice–let it happen. As Benny said to Smalls, (because it's worth repeating–and you should!): "You gotta stop thinking." (David Mickey Evans and Gunter 1993).

The Science of the Mind

There are doctors and scientists who focus exclusively on the function of the mind, especially those of athletes. They make up the branch of psychology known–not surprisingly–as Sports Psychology.

Sports psychology has been around for quite a while. One instance occurred in 1898, when psychologist Norman Triplett studied the behavior of professional cyclists and determined that those who rode in teams performed better than those who cycled alone–probably because teams fulfilled their natural social and competitive needs. In 1925, the first lab devoted to sports psychology was opened. Still, it wasn't until 1965 that the International Society of Sport Psychology (ISSP) was established. (Sports Psychology History n.d.)

In the 1980s (100 years after Triplett's study), researchers began to explore how this branch of psychology could be used to improve athletic performance; as a result, new branches and specialties of sports psychology were created.

Educational sports psychologists use their training to help athletes improve their in-game performance by using techniques like imagery, goal setting, and self-talk. They teach skills to help athletes compete better and win more games. This book is an example of an educational sports psychology tool.

Sports psychologists focus on training athletes to understand and play "the inner game" by teaching them to set goals, visualize positive outcomes, manage the ways they talk to themselves, and, above all, giving them ways to do their best on–and off–the playing field (Jenkins 2020).

Meanwhile, **clinical sports psychologists** are more highly-trained than educational sports psychologists; they focus on the mental health of athletes, helping them to work through issues like depression and anxiety by combining sports psychology and general psychotherapy.

The benefits of sports psychology include things like:

- Reduced anxiety
- Mental toughness

- Effective stress management techniques
- An increased drive to perform
- A healthier perspective of yourself and your abilities

Let's say, for example, that you're a high school basketball player. You're not content with just playing—you have incredibly high expectations for your performance. Some people might even say that you're a perfectionist. You're great at the game—until you make a mistake. Once that happens, you're toast. You spend the rest of your time on the floor thinking about that mistake. As a result, you miss shots...and get more upset with yourself. You doubt your abilities, instead focusing on your missed opportunity. This turns into missed opportunities as you cycle into a spiral of "I suck."

Or maybe you're a baseball player. You're a pretty good hitter—until you're not. Nothing is as dreaded as the slump; coaches and professional players alike can attest to how striking out during one time up can lead to striking out a second time, and then a third, and then fourth...and then the game is over. You're left to think about how the baseball started to look as small as a pea flying over the plate into the catcher's glove with a resounding "smack," and the way the bat seemed to move as if you were swinging through molasses, never making contact. You work on your mechanics, but it doesn't seem to be that you're doing anything different than what you always did–except not hitting. You get anxious before the next game, convinced the same thing is going to happen...and it usually does. Unless you can get out of your head, you might be stuck in your slump for a long time.

These are situations where you need sports psychology, and, in fact, both of these examples are real situations experienced by real athletes who used its techniques and principles in order to get out of their heads and back into the game (Cohn 2012).

Working it Out:

Before we get into this first exercise, an explanation. At the end of every chapter, I'm going to provide an exercise for you to do. This will probably involve some kind of writing, and it may even feel like homework.

Doing these exercises is not required, of course. That being said, if you really want to grow and maintain confidence and focus, understand your anxiety, and use visualization to dominate in your sport, you're going to need to do more than just read. Think of the exercises I provide as another form of practice to build your athletic skills.

You'll need to do some deep digging into your psyche. Keep in mind, however, that whatever you write isn't anything you need to share (unless you want to show it to someone you trust). It doesn't have to be pretty. Also, if you don't want to write in this book (where someone might see your thoughts), you can write your reflections on a separate piece of paper and then hide it somewhere safe. Or, if you want, you can write your thoughts on your phone.

And if the thought of writing is really just too awful, you can video your answers and reflections for these exercises on camera and save them. (Just be careful not to accidentally upload them to your favorite social media site!)

CHAPTER EXERCISE #1: REFRAMING

Think about an incident during your athletic career, or even during a class at school, that had a negative impact on your performance.

Live that moment over again, and experience–once more–the way it made you feel. Whatever happened then, it's important not to judge yourself for the outcome now. What you're focusing on is the emotions you had and the physical reactions that occurred as well. And then think about how you can change what you did—and how you'll do it—in order to create success the next time. This is called *reframing*.

When you reframe a situation, you look at it differently so that you can improve on it. It doesn't mean to sugar-coat the situation or try to convince yourself that the outcome was different. You still realize that it wasn't the best situation, especially if you failed or messed up. However, you take the judgment out of your feedback and look for ways to adapt it for improvement.

Let me give you an example. It's not an athletic situation, but it's something I think anyone who is reading this book can relate to; this book is written for athletes of every sport—besides competition, one thing all of us have in common is academics.

In my 10th-grade history class, we had to give a five-minute speech about a historical figure and their most major accomplishment. I got an F on my speech and ruined my GPA. It was the most embarrassing thing that happened to me that year.

I could feel my face was hot and red. I thought I was going to choke, and my heart pounded so hard I shook all over. Worse, my mouth dried up and I practically lost my voice!

For a long time, I avoided thinking about that incident; whenever I did, I was embarrassed all over again. I thought things like, "I can't talk in front of people," and "I'm an idiot. I don't know how to do research..." and "I hate Benjamin Franklin." (Poor Ben. It wasn't his fault he got assigned to me.)

I could have decided "I suck at public speaking" and freaked out every time I needed to give a speech or presentation in the future. But instead of criticizing myself into silence, I gave myself honest, non-judgmental feedback: "I could have done a better job."

From there, all I had to do was determine what a "better job" would be and how I could make that happen. For one thing, I realized I should have brought some water to the podium with me so that when my mouth grew dry, I could take a drink, wet my mouth and throat, and be able to keep talking.

I also could have practiced ahead of time to make sure my speech would actually fill the whole five minutes and not be over in thirty seconds. I didn't realize that once I started, I'd get so nervous I'd talk too fast!

Once I was able to take the emotion and judgment out of my high school public speaking experience, I was able to plan ahead for my next public speaking experience in college. Yes, I was nervous and, yes my heart pounded so hard my entire body shook (again). But, this time, I had that bottle of water so my throat didn't go dry.

I'm glad I did because every time I took a drink, it gave me a chance to rest between note cards, to gather my thoughts, and take a deep calming breath. That helped me to slow down so that my speech was timed almost perfectly. On this occasion, I received an A. In fact, I discovered I actually *enjoyed* public speaking.

Now it's your turn. What "failure" can you use to reframe for growth so that you can do it better in the future?

2

UNDERSTANDING YOUR PREGAME ANXIETY

"Never let the fear of striking out get in your way."

— *BASEBALL LEGEND GEORGE HERMAN*
"BABE" RUTH

You're in the locker room, suiting up, and you've got the sweats. Your stomach is churning. Your heart is pounding, your limbs are shaking, and you're afraid you're going to vomit. Welcome to the world of pregame jitters!

It doesn't matter what level of athleticism you're at, varsity or professional, you can be affected by anxiety before your game. This is a normal and very common feeling. In fact, if it makes you feel better, think about Andrew McLeod. McLeod played for The Adelaide Crows Football Club in the Australian Football League, a champion with over 300 games. Without fail, he threw up before *every* match. In spite of that–and maybe, because of it–he is considered one of the best, most consistent Aussie Rules Football Players ever (Athlete IQ, 2020).

So you're not alone. The basketball players who just claimed their fourth championship in eight years; the boxer who had just successfully defended his title for the nineteenth time; the quarterback who calmly moves his team to the end zone again and again–all of them have experienced, continue to experience, and will *always* experience pregame anxiety. It's practically a part of the game. Whether you experience it every game or not, you can prepare how you'll deal with it if it occurs, and–good news!–be confident that you don't have to let it affect you in a negative way.

There's a reason you feel this way. It means you *care* about the game you're going to play, or the competition you're about to enter, and you're concerned about the outcome. Think about it–if you didn't care, and it didn't matter whether you won or lost–then you probably wouldn't feel anything.

In a way, that would be worse. You'd be indifferent, nonchalant, blase...bored. But no, you're excited, and this game matters to you. It could be that you and your teammates have practiced hard. Or maybe you're an athlete who competes alone; it could be playing tennis, doing gymnastics, diving, or skating. You've spent hours preparing for the moment that's about to occur. And you know that once you enter the arena, all eyes will be on you–there will be no second chances. You have to care. Why else would you bother playing? Football legend and quarterback, Joe Namath put it best: "If you aren't going all the way, why go at all?" You're here to go all the way and that can cause anxiety.

UNDERSTANDING PREGAME ANXIETY

Human beings tend to focus on the future (and results) instead of the present. This makes sense; if human beings didn't plan for the future (especially when we relied on growing food and hunting), we wouldn't survive. But along with focusing on the future comes fear because we can't predict what's going to happen with any certainty.

So we predict what we think will happen. Unfortunately–for some reason–human beings also tend to focus on the negative. Maybe because it's part of planning for an especially long winter; if we didn't worry about having enough food/water, survival wouldn't happen either. It makes sense–if you're a cave dweller.

Move this same method of thought to modern times, and you've got humanity now. We're all anxious and when we get into a success or fail situation, we're tighter than an elastic band stretched and ready to snap. Scientists say that we're actually dealing with anxiety and one other issue: arousal. Anxiety, of course, is emotional and psychological. As I've been saying–it's all in our heads. Arousal, on the other hand, is physical. When we're in a state of arousal (or alertness), our coordination and muscles are all on high alert and our focus is all around us.

Have you ever had the opportunity to watch a wild rabbit munching on a lawn? It's anything but a relaxing dining experience for the poor bunny. The whole time they're trying to get in a mouthful of fresh grass, they're looking around wide-eyed, with their ears twitching every which way. (It's a wonder they don't feel like *they're* going to throw up. Maybe they do; we'll never know.) At any rate, they're aroused, alert, and waiting to be eaten. Or to run.

Another name for this is the *fight or flight response*. Rabbits usually run; it's not often they'll fight unless there's a good reason. (If you go on YouTube, you can find some badass bunnies duking it out with dogs and cats and other predators. Warning! They usually lose.) The point is, human beings in tense situations are just like those rabbits; they're ready to run, fight or freeze. While you'd think this state of arousal will make your body ready to react to anything, it sometimes has the opposite effect–making you tense up to the point of being almost paralyzed. (Just like a scared bunny.) You're stuck listening to your racing, negative thoughts (I doubt the rabbit has negative thoughts beyond, "I'm going to be eaten!", but anything's possible...).

Symptoms of Pregame Anxiety

While the symptoms are different for every athlete, in general, you'll experience all or some of the following:

- Poor concentration/lack or loss of focus
- Thoughts or images of failure
- Loss of confidence
- Increased or pounding heart
- Sweating
- Dry mouth
- Trembling/uncontrolled shaking
- Tight muscles
- "Butterflies in the stomach"
- Inability to meet other's eyes/avoiding eye contact
- Excessive talking or an inability to talk

- A desire to play it safe/lack of, or loss of confidence
- Cognitive symptoms, or thought processes, include fear, indecision, loss of confidence, poor concentration, images of failure, thoughts of avoidance.
- Physical symptoms include increased blood pressure, pounding heart, sweating, dry mouth, trembling, muscular tension, butterflies in the stomach.
- Behavioral symptoms include avoidance of eye contact, biting the fingernails, introversion or excessive extroversion, "playing it safe" (Gloveworx 2018).

As horrible as these symptoms are for you in that moment, they're not the worst thing that can happen. In fact, you can use these reactions to succeed at your game instead of letting them overwhelm you. We'll talk about this further on.

OVERCOMING PREGAME ANXIETY

Let's call it like it is: anxiety sucks. Some people get so upset by their anxiety, they have anxiety about their anxiety! But it doesn't have to be that way. There are things you can do to minimize your anxiety at the time you're experiencing it and even stop it before it occurs.

1) Talk to Yourself

For some people, it's as easy as engaging in conversation with yourself and doing a little "self-talk." You probably do this already, especially if you're already anxious; you may even say things to yourself like "I suck" or "I'm going to miss every shot I take" or "I'm going to throw up and they'll have to delay the game and everyone will call me 'Puker' for the rest of my life."

Thinking that way isn't very helpful. Negative self-talk like this will only make you play badly and derail your self-confidence.

What you need to do is engage in *positive* self-talk. Tell yourself things like, "I did great in practice and I can do great here" or "I wouldn't have made the team if I didn't have what it takes" or even more simply, "I've got what it takes!"

It's generally accepted that positive self-talk can greatly reduce anxiety. Benefits will almost certainly include:

- Greater confidence
- Less anxiety symptoms
- Better performance

2) Listen to Music

It's probably not surprising to you that listening to music can make a big difference in how you feel. Scientists and nonscientists alike have recognized how music can affect us; for generations, people have soothed babies with lullabies and serenaded potential love interests with ballads. Music matters.

In most cases, the type of music you choose to listen to before a game doesn't matter; as long as it's something you like it can be relaxing or nonrelaxing. However, a 2017 study discovered that students considered to be "elite shooters" performed better at their games after listening to what the researchers considered "non relaxing" music (Elliott, Polman, and Taylor 2012).

You'll have to give it a try to see what kind of music affects you more—you want to listen to something that calms your anxiety and helps you to focus without making you less effective at your sport.

3) Meditation

Meditation is a way to calm and relax the mind and body by developing and using focus techniques on the brain, the body, the mind, and behavior ("NCCIH," n.d.). It's something you'll want to do before a game or anytime you find yourself feeling particularly anxious. (Anytime except *during* a game, unless you can find a quiet place to sit for a bit. If you participate in a solo sport that's not timed, you might try to meditate for focus just before your event.)

There are many ways to meditate, but one really simple and easy one that you can use anywhere is called *focused attention meditation*. This teaches you to focus entirely on one thing–a word, an item you see, or a sound (like birdsong, or water flowing), which gives you a chance to stop your thoughts from racing. Some people focus on their breathing.

If you want to give this a try, choose something. Let's go with a visual, something random. Like...a water bottle.

1. Look at it. By that, I mean, *really* look at it. The shape of it, its color, how it reflects light if it's clear, or the logo if it has one. Is it shiny or dull? Does it have a texture or is it smooth?
2. Keep your attention–your focus–on that bottle. You can even think of the word "bottle".
3. If you find your attention wandering or your thoughts starting to go off (and they will, at first), gently bring them back to focus.

4. After some time–and practice–you will find
   this easier to do.

There are many paid and free apps you can try, and if you Google "meditation", you'll find a variety of videos and articles with suggestions and how-to's. Searching through these can help you to find the technique and type of meditation that works best for you.

4) Visualization

Visualization is sometimes called *imagery*; this is a good name for it because it involves using your imagination to eliminate negative thoughts or ideas and to calm yourself in stressful or anxiety-causing situations ("Information from Your Patient Aligned Care Team Visualization/Guided Imagery," n.d.). Professionals call it *visualization*, however–so that's what I'll use here.

Visualization is effective because our minds don't recognize the difference between what's real and what's imaginary (Hamilton 2019). Many professional athletes use it to "practice" prior to a big game, where they imagine they are successful. If you do this, you'll be able to trick your mind into releasing feel-good hormones instead of the ones that make you anxious.

Using visualization is similar to meditation; it's something that requires a quiet, restful place to sit–preferably someplace where you can be alone without distractions. So you'll want to use this technique prior to game time, not during a game. You'll want to be able to sit comfortably and safely with your eyes closed.

Once you're sitting still with your eyes closed, start imagining a place (your "happy place") that is peaceful and relaxing to you. It can be a place you've been, or it could be a place that exists only in your imagination. You can imagine yourself on a beach, on a mountain, deep in the woods or in a park, or even indoors on a comfy couch in front of a crackling fire with snow lashing against the windows.

What sounds do you hear? Notice how I mentioned a "crackling" fire; that's a sound description. In your happy place, what do you hear? The more details you can conjure up in your happy place that appeal to your five senses, the more effective this technique will be.

Let's try it. We'll use a beach (since that's my happy place). Sometimes it's recommended that once you're seated and comfortable with your eyes closed that you "walk" yourself to your destination as part of the experience. Or, you can just plop yourself there. But for this exercise, let's walk.

You find yourself on a road; a short distance away is a wooden boardwalk across sandy dunes. Beside it, beach grass shivers and dances in the wind. The sun is bright–almost too bright, but you can handle it. Or maybe you've got a set of sunglasses in your pocket or a hat with a visor that you can use to shade your eyes. You step onto the boardwalk. Maybe you decide to take off your shoes so you can feel the hot, rough boards under your feet, or maybe you're wearing sandals or sneakers so you don't feel those boards, but you can hear the dull thud they make as you move along it, over the dunes, to see a quiet, secluded beach below.

The water is a deep-blue color, and sunlight sparkles over the waves. You step down onto the sand, sinking slightly because it's soft. You can feel the muscles in your thighs and calves contracting because of the sandy surface; it feels good. You feel strong. You walk down closer to the water, and finally, you sit down.

The waves are rolling in and out; they land on the beach with a crash and a boom, then pull away with a hiss and a sizzle. Seagulls cry overhead. The wind whistles in from the water. How does it feel? Is it a warm wind or a cool one? Does it mess up your hair and make it tickle your skin? Does it carry the scent of salt and maybe sunscreen? If you're sitting on the sand how does it feel? Is it soft and fine, or is it rocky and rough?

You might even decide to go for a swim!

Breathe deeply and soak in the peace you feel in this place. Whatever thoughts occur to you, notice them, but let them go like a fish into the sea or a kite on the wind. And keep bringing your focus back to your place, noticing the details, and enjoying the peace that comes with it.

There's no set time for this technique; you can remain in your happy place for a few minutes or longer. Once you're ready to leave, you can stand and walk back to the road, leaving the image behind, but not the feeling of calm it provided. Enjoy how any tension or stress you were feeling has faded while you restored your mind with visualization.

Another truly effective technique is to use imagery to picture yourself in a game situation–winning, and anxiety-free. Visualizing success is something many professional athletes do before a game. Use the same method I showed you above; be as detailed as possible.

Here are some other techniques related to visualization that you can try:

1. **Blue light technique:** This is similar to meditation and visualization. But instead of visualizing your happy place, you imagine that

you're in the center of a calm, blue light. Inhale and visualize the blue light filling your body. Exhale and imagine the anxiety you're feeling leaving you as a dark smoke so that the light can fill you completely. Continue a few more times, breathing deeply in, and then out. What this method does is make you slow down and stop focusing on your panic and anxiety by focusing on your breathing instead.

2. **Stop It:** This technique is especially helpful if you're the kind of person who *perseverates* (a fancy word that means to repeat something over and over again for no real reason). If you find that your thoughts are stuck on a particular topic, or if you're continually imagining failure or a terrible outcome, psychologists recommend you visualize a big red stop sign. As you stop to consider this sign, ask yourself, "Is thinking this way helping me, or is it making me feel worse?" Chances are, you're just making yourself more anxious. The stop sign is a way to get you to divert your panic and *stop!* making yourself anxious.

3. **Be the one you want to be:** When you were little, you may have imagined yourself being a superhero, or your favorite character in a movie or on tv. This technique is similar and

just as fun. All you need to do is imagine yourself being your favorite, most admired athlete. How would they approach the field? How would they handle this situation, and how would they overcome this obstacle? Doing this might feel a *little-kid-ish*, but it helps you to realize that even great athletes have been where you are; they just managed to overcome it. You can too! (Hims, n.d.)

Pregame Rituals to Stop Anxiety

It's game time, and your mind is racing. Are you ready? Are you going to perform well? What if...? What about...? We already know this is the result of pregame anxiety, and that you can use one, several, or all of the techniques above to help you combat it. But there's one other technique that is so effective, it deserves its own section.

It's called a *pregame ritual.* In case you're unsure what a ritual is, here's the definition: a *ritual* is a ceremony or action performed in a customary way. So a pregame ritual is something you do–in a familiar or customary way–before a game to help you focus, or gain composure and/or the confidence you need to get you ready to perform at peak.

Dr. Thomas Newmark of the International Society of Sports Psychiatrists explains, "Most athletes...have little rituals and superstitions that they do. [Games] are filled with elements beyond your control. Rituals, lucky charms, and superstitions give you little things you can control. It's something you can do that is familiar and soothing that can help you control anxiety ... and to that end, maybe perform better (Yeager, 2011)."

Here are some rituals and superstitions from professional athletes past and present:

1. Tony Jefferson of the Baltimore Ravens likes to watch an episode of his favorite show (Ferber 2017).
2. Detroit Pistons' Nerlens Noel put it this way, "Nothing too crazy with me, I just have my own little preparation — I got my headphones and get ready in my own zone. I'm not really joking around too much," he says. "But I always get the butterflies. Always."
3. American hurdler and sprinter, Sydney McLaughlin, doesn't exactly have a ritual, but she does have a lucky blanket that she takes to—and uses–at every meet.
4. When Zaza Puchulia played for the Golden State Warriors (now he's in the front office), he would take a nap, then eat carbs before every

game. His carb of choice: Pasta with one of several different sauces but not the same one in a row.

5. Steven John "Turk" Wendell, a former relief pitcher for the New York Mets, had one of the most elaborate rituals - it was quite superstitiously quirky. He'd always hop over the baselines when heading to the mound *and* he'd brush his teeth between every inning.

Pregame rituals work because they give you something to focus on right now. Instead of worrying or being anxious about what's going to happen during the game–something over which you have no control–a ritual is something you can control. It helps take away the anxiety and puts you in the present.

Developing Your Own Pregame Ritual

There are many ways to create your own pregame routine or ritual; keep in mind that very few athletes will have the same ritual. But the ways to establish those routines will be similar for most.

Two specific phases occur in a pregame ritual. The first phase occurs the night–or maybe even a few days–before your event, and the second phase happens just before the event. You will be using techniques to help you be your best athlete, and working to relax, build your confidence, and hone your focus so that you won't be distracted internally or externally.

1) Phase One:

This is all about mental preparation. For this phase, you'll want to get as much information as you can about your opposition. One good way to do this is by watching videos about your opponent. Some high schools hire videographers to record every game and upload it online. Sometimes family and friends of your competition share videos. Find them and watch them! By doing so, you can find any weaknesses, patterns, and tendencies that will give you an edge.

Five times Superbowl QB Tom Brady puts it this way: "...the more I prepare, the less nervous I get because I can kind of expect how things are going to go a little bit more if I have a little more information on the team. So the more film I watch, the less nervous I get (Anderson 2019)."

There are many ways to watch videos for insight into your opponent's plays and playing style. Some players take notes as they watch, just as they would at school, using an open Google doc or a notebook (Doc Bear 2015). The reason for this is twofold: one, you can go back and re-read your notes later when you might not have access to your device, and two, notes force you to pay attention and help to reinforce what you're seeing. Writing things down while seeing them is like seeing them more than once; you will remember them more easily.

When you watch film, don't sit there passively. You might even want to go into the exercise with a specific plan. Some experts recommend that you don't watch the ball (or puck); instead, concentrate on the player you will be up against. That makes sense; a puck is just an inanimate object - it's the opposing player you're analyzing. What are their habits? How do they move? What chinks do they have in their armor that you can exploit?

Watch the video in slow motion, if possible. Rewind, rewatch, repeat. Focus in on everything you can. You're not watching for pleasure or for fun. You're watching to win–give yourself the serious edge.

Once you've collected your insight into your opponents, go someplace quiet where you can do some mental practice. You're going to use your imagination once more. Let me walk you through this using my friend's experience as a high school baseball player as an example.

A high school friend of mine once told me that batting is the skill where he found himself the most stressed, probably because, as skilled as he was, there was much outside his direct control. His method of coping with the stress was through visualization. He'd begin by "walking" himself into the on-deck circle. As you should for visualization, he'd imagine the scene using all of his senses–sight, sound, hearing, smell, and physical feeling. He'd even feel his muscles bunching and shifting as he swung the bat and felt his weight shifting in his feet, feel the weight of the bat in his hands, hear the woosh of the bat through the air, the sounds of people in the stands, maybe the cheering from the game going on in one of the other fields at the facility, smell the scent of the grass, and maybe the hot dogs and burgers being grilled at the concession stands...After that, he'd leave the on-deck circle and step into the batter's box, where he'd go through his usual ritual of tapping the plate and swinging–three times– to relax while watching the pitcher at the mound.

Then he would imagine himself hitting every pitch he could face. He'd go even further by creating stressful situations like a full count with the bases loaded to bring his team ahead–with all pressure to succeed on his shoulders. He'd make up situations like this over and over again, with success each time.

From there, he would move on to defense, where he'd successfully field balls in—you guessed it—clutch situations. Each time he did this, he'd feel the stress of the moment and the triumphant joy of success as well. Once he'd moved himself around the field and placed himself in multiple stressful situations, he'd relax, get his gear ready for the ballfield and make sure his uniform was all set so he wouldn't have stress trying to find something before gametime. He'd take time to get Gatorade in the fridge to put in the cooler before the game. And then—most importantly—he'd be sure to get a good night's rest.

2) Phase Two:

Game day! Today, your routine needs to be about being relaxed and focused on success. Because fear of failure is one of the primary reasons we suffer from pregame anxiety, the anticipation of success is the best way to combat it. So if you find yourself getting anxious, remember your phase one scenarios and the success you imagined. Tom Brady says, "...as soon as the ball's kicked off, there's not too many nerves (Anderson 2019)."

You can use the other techniques discussed above to help you fight your nerves: listen to music, meditate, visualize—whatever you find most helpful to get yourself out of your head and back into your game. Try all of them out–one at a time, or a combination of them–to create your own routine and methods of reducing or eliminating your pregame anxiety.

CHAPTER EXERCISE #2: KEEPING A RECORD

This is something you can do again and again, and use it as an opportunity to understand your pregame anxiety and how to overcome it. Do this by writing 3 physical goals and also, 3 mental goals for your game. After the game, go back and write how you were successful in completing each goal during your event. I know it might seem silly or perhaps even a waste of time to keep a journal-type record; after all, this is real life, not school. (And I understand–you've probably been keeping journals and writing things like this since kindergarten.) But there's a reason for them, and a good one! Keeping a record–for yourself–isn't just something you do for a grade or for busy work. Instead, it can actually be the difference between never achieving your full potential or *excelling* to your next level of performance. You don't have to share it with anyone but yourself; it doesn't have to be pretty to look at, follow a particular format, or reach a certain word count. What it does need to do is give you a place to mark where you started, how you achieved, and how you succeed. Later, you can go back and see how far you've come and be motivated to do even more.

Defining your success makes you focus on success during your game—which keeps you from worrying about failure. Writing about it after and keeping a record will help you to realize you *are* successful, which takes your attention off the anxiety and fear of failure in the future.

Ultimately, this is the result of mental imagery for sports success. This is so important for your sports success—and even in other areas of your life! We're going to go more deeply into this topic in the next chapter.

3

AN IN-DEPTH LOOK AT THE SCIENCE OF SPORTS VISUALIZATION

"Visualization is the human being's vehicle to the future- good, bad or indifferent."

— *EARL NIGHTINGALE (KNOWN AS THE "DEAN OF PERSONAL DEVELOPMENT")*

In the previous chapter, we saw that one of the ways to control pregame anxiety is through visualization. It turns out that visualization, or imagery, can also apply to other aspects of sports, like building skills and increasing your chances of success.

Back in the 1970s, the then-Soviet Union's athletes began using it as a method of mental practice. Since that time, the technique has become common as part of training programs for athletes of all sports, and for other professionals too. Its effects are so well-recognized that only a few—mostly unsuccessful people—consider visualization some kind of gimmick. Everyone else, from billionaires to Olympic gold medalists and high-earning coaches for big-name teams, knows better. Even golf legend Tiger Woods has been using sports visualization since before he was a teenager (Adams 2009). So when it comes to the credibility of the effectiveness of sports (or performance) visualization, which "side" do you think you should believe?

The winning side, of course!

WHAT IS SPORTS VISUALIZATION?

Physiologist Edmund Jacobson performed an experiment where he asked his subjects to visualize their athletic activities. While they visualized, he used sensitive detection devices on them and found that their muscles made subtle but real movements that corresponded to the same ones they'd make if actually being used (Randolph 2002).

Later, a different psychologist named Alan Richardson confirmed this phenomenon by creating a study using three groups of randomly chosen volunteers, none of whom had ever practiced visualization. In the first group, the volunteers practiced free throws every day for twenty days. The second and third group of volunteers did not physically practice any free throws during the study, but the third group was instructed to visualize shooting free throws. In their visualization, if they visualized missing the throws, they'd also visually practice getting the next shot right and perfect.

At the end of the study, on the twentieth day, Richardson measured the percentage of improvement in each group. He discovered a 24% improvement in the group that practiced daily. In the second group that did not physically or mentally practice–not surprisingly–there was no improvement at all. But the third group who had performed the same number of physical throws as the second group mentally were found to have improved by 23%, almost as much as the group which had practiced free throws daily. Which is crazy to think they were able to improve their skill, by just *thinking*!

This study gives hope to athletes who may have become injured and have been sidelined during their recuperation period. While they may be on crutches or in a cast, they can't work out with the rest of the team. But as long as they can visualize, they can–in a sense–continue to work out with the team and potentially keep their skills strong on the sidelines until they're cleared to go back to the field.

In the previous chapter, I showed you several exercises where you can use imagination to create scenarios—successful ones—in your mind. I discussed how important it is to use all of your senses in your visualizations so that they're as real as possible. This is important because studies have shown that mental imagery produces the same effect in the brain as physical actions. Motor control, attention and focus, perception, planning, and even memory are affected by this technique. When you intentionally visualize your actions, you're training your brain and—in a sense, your body—because *your brain doesn't know the difference between what's real and what you've made up* (Adams 2009)!

Don't worry if you're not great at using your imagination; scientists have found that anyone can develop visualization skills if they practice performing mental rehearsals. Some experts suggest practice should "last at least one minute but never exceed five minutes" (Predoiu 2020); others feel that the length of time doesn't matter as much as being consistent with your visualization. Others adhere to the idea that your visualization should take as long as the actual action to complete. But none of them agree on the best amount of time for maximum effectiveness; it's possible that's because everyone is different. Ultimately, then, it's up to you to decide what works best for you as regards the time you spend.

The most important thing to try to remember is to include as many sensory details as possible; this is why I included so many details during my sample visualization from when my friend played baseball.

Psychologists also suggest trying different *imagery perspectives*. Imagery perspective is how you see when you create your visualizations. Some people are more comfortable seeing the situation from the inside looking out (as in life); others like to see themselves performing externally as if watching themselves on a video. Either way works–again, it's unique for everyone because everyone has a different point of view (Taylor 2012).

Another thing to use in your visualizations is the environment. If you're playing football in November in the Northeastern US, chances are it's going to be cold. In fact, there might be a forecast for snow; include that in your pregame visualizations and create some scenarios where it might affect your playing. Of course, then you'll imagine yourself successful as you play in the snow. Visualizing the reality of your future event will make a BIG difference in your performance.

Benefits of Sports Visualization

Scientists have determined that motivation, motor skills, and confidence can be improved just by visualizing success in sports performance. These other benefits include:

- Increased focus of attention
- Increased confidence on (and off) the playing field
- Thoughts become more disciplined
- Abilities improve
- Motivation is enhanced
- Recovery time improves

Remember what I said about how the brain can't tell the difference between what you imagine and what is real? The same thing applies to healing; it has been found that visualizing an injury healing actually helps it to improve. Further, chronic pain and headaches can be lessened or even eliminated (Weiland 2016).

Visualization is so powerful I continue to use it as an adult when I have a situation where my performance is paramount. In fact, professionals in many occupations use visualization to help them do their job better, from surgeons who need to complete delicate, life-saving procedures, to motivational speakers who need to address large crowds, from astronauts who need to leave their ships to perform technical actions in a limited amount of time–in outer space!--to musicians who need to play a solo piece in an orchestra. There's no doubt that performance visualization is a great tool for success in many professions.

For an athlete–or anybody–one of the best things about visualization is that while you can't control the outcome of every game in real life, by using imagery you are always in control. The only thing you'll do in your "head game" is win.

HOW TO VISUALIZE

1-Set a Goal:

Sports psychologists recommend going into your visualization with a goal. This makes sense; you could wander around in your visualization accomplishing nothing. Having something to achieve in your visualization to succeed *at* will bring you the success you want. So be it tactical, technical, skill-related, or related to your state of mind, make sure that you know what you're trying to achieve in your visualization to bring you the most success.

2-Find a Comfortable Place:

Most articles and experts don't mention this, but it's kind of important. If you're not comfortable in your reality, how are you going to create success in your imagination? Find a comfortable place and position–just don't be so comfortable that you end up falling asleep! (Although if you do fall asleep, it probably means you probably needed the rest!)

3-Breathe:

You've got your goal, you've got your comfortable position. Now you need to breathe. Take in a deep breath in (preferably in through your nose). Let it out slowly (preferably out of your mouth). Repeat a few more times. This will signal your body that you're doing something different, and it will help you to relax so you can focus. As above, however, don't fall asleep!

4-Visualize:

Stay focused on your performance and skills, practicing in your mind the skills and techniques you learned in your practices. For example, if you play football, think about a play you might have practiced. Look at it from all points of view and places on the field. How would your opponent see it? Where are you supposed to be on the field and what is your role? How will you make this play a success? How can you come through in the clutch? Do this for as long as you'd like, but do it thoroughly.

5-Create a Routine:

Just like practice for your sport improves your athletic skills, practicing visualization improves your visualization skills. And just like you physically practice several times a week, you need to mentally practice to make it perfect.

You don't have to do your visualizations all at the same time, especially when you're first starting. Just like you don't run a marathon on the first day, you work up to longer sessions bit by bit.

Motivational speaker, Brian Tracy, puts it this way: *"Winners make a habit of manufacturing their own positive expectations in advance of the event."* Make the creation of your own pregame positive expectations into a habit!

6-Keep a Journal:

I know, I know. Honestly, I can hear your groans from here. Keeping a journal may feel just like homework. So let me say this: It's up to you whether or not you want to keep a visualization journal, but the reason for it is simple and important. In fact, I really want you to keep one—again, this is the difference between being good and being clutch!

Being clutch doesn't happen instantly; it takes work, and that means work off the playing field or out of the arena or rink. Sometimes it means time spent at the gym, and in this case, some time at your desk or wherever you choose to write. In fact, I challenge you to try it for a month. Put it on your calendar, a daily task At the end of the thirty days of honest and sincere effort (not just scribbling something, but putting in the work), I can guarantee almost 100% that you will be able to see an honest difference, and that comes from keeping a journal. In addition, by keeping a record of your progress, you can easily see the results of your visualization. In the end, sports are about results–stats matter. By keeping track of what imagery may have worked–or didn't work!--you'll have a better idea of how to visualize in your next session. You can also use a journal to record the length of your visualization sessions and know for sure how often you used visualization. Plus, you'll be able to record how you felt before, during, and after each session for your future self.

A journal will also enable you to create a list of potential scenarios to imagine. And, as you write, you will automatically be visualizing–so it will serve a dual purpose and reinforce your visualization. Or, it can be a place to write positive things for yourself to think about like, "I am a strong athlete," "I have game," or even, "I am clutch."

Record-Holding Athletes Who Use Visualization

Some of the world's top athletes of all time used visualization to reach the pinnacle of their sport. What can you learn from them?

1- Michael Phelps

There is no denying that Michael Phelps is the most successful Olympian of all time and holds the record for the most medals ever won (23 gold medals, plus 3 silver and 2 bronze). He learned sports visualization from his coach, Bob Bowman. Every night before he goes to sleep, Phelps visualizes a race with a successful outcome. He does this again in the morning when he wakes up. His visualizations include every detail of the race, from the starting block to the celebration when he wins (LaBorde 2019).

2-Katie Ledecky

Katie Ledecky, like Phelps, is a world-record-holding swimmer, with 6 Olympic individual gold medals and 14 world championship individual gold medals, the most ever for a female swimmer. Ledecky says: "I have my goals and I visualize things to help me achieve those goals ... I know what my stroke should feel like at different parts of the race, and I can just kind of picture that in my mind (Rovello 2016)."

A Recap About Visualization

Just to sum it up: Visualization works!

- Visualize often and consistently. Make it part of your practice routine.
- Use images from either your internal point of view (1st person), or externally (3rd person) as if you're watching yourself perform successfully.
- Be detailed, and use all of your five senses.
- Set goals about what you want to achieve during a game or event and visualize yourself achieving them.
- Keep a record for your future self.

There is one thing that I haven't touched on in this chapter—probably because it's something that seems obvious. But just in case you think that doing visualization is a way to skip out of practice and hard work (and it would be great if that was true), remember this: Visualization—although an effective tool in achieving your sports goals—is *not* a replacement for physical practice. As much as it's been proven to be a means to make you be clutch, you still need to show up, do the work, and be ready to compete!

CHAPTER EXERCISE #3: PUTTING IT INTO PRACTICE

Simply put–try it out. The only way to get good at visualization is through practice. Now's the time, when the pressure is off, to try to visualize yourself performing a skill or task successfully. Give yourself time and have fun with it. Remember–you are the one in control, and you are able to make yourself be as successful as you want yourself to be. The only limitations you have are the ones you create for yourself - so don't create any.

When you're done, write about it. Tell yourself (your future self) what you visualized and how it made you feel. Make sure you mark the time you spent visualizing, what time of day it is, and whether or not you felt successful in visualizing. Then, make a plan for the next time. Pretty soon, visualization will be a good habit that will be hard to break–setting and keeping goals is the way to make that happen.

Speaking of goal setting...in our next two chapters, we'll be discussing the connection between visualization and goal setting, and how to use each to enhance the other for explosive athletic performance to make you *be* clutch.

4

A YOUNG ATHLETE'S GUIDE TO SETTING GOALS

"Goals determine what you're going to be."

— *"DR. J", JULIUS ERVING (BASKETBALL GREAT)*

To get into the clutch mindset, you need to have a goal. Without it, competing would be purposeless, and actions would have no direction. In sports, winning your event is the overall goal, but to get there, you need to plan smaller milestones that create a sense of achievement. Make sure, however, that each milestone you achieve is a step towards your final goal.

WHY GOALS?

Why *not* goals is probably the better question. Goals are important in any part of life. We have goals for our grades, for our college aspirations, for our careers, for our finances–just about everything you do, every day, occurs because you had an initial goal. Even if it was something as mundane as taking a nap or eating a sandwich; you decided it was something you needed to do, and you acted on the steps you needed to take to make it happen.

As an athlete, goals are especially important.

- Goals give you a reason to push yourself
- Goals motivate you to overcome obstacles
- Goals help you to determine your focus
- Goals show you where your skill level needs to be

The Three Types of Goals

Generally speaking, three different types of goals are recognized by sports psychologists:

1-Outcome goals. These goals are what you ultimately wish to achieve during your performance.

2- **Process goals.** These give you a target for *what* you will do to achieve your desired outcome. What is your process for success? These are generally considered short-term goals because they apply to a specific event or game.

3-**Performance goals.** These give you a target for *how* you want to perform, or what you will do during your event to achieve your outcome goal. These are generally considered mid-term goals and can be used to track the improvement of your skills.

How to Set Sports Goals

A quick search on the word "goals" will lead you to lots of articles and videos from Olympic athletes. There are very few, and, in fact, possibly no Olympians who don't set goals for their performance. Here's what some of these elite athletes say about goals (keep in mind that some of their advice may seem contradictory, but that's pretty standard for human nature; use the ideas that work for you and ignore the rest):

- *Your goals need to be specific enough to measure.*
  Think about it. You won't hear any athlete say that they want to "run faster." Instead, they'll say they want to beat a specific time, go a particular distance, or be in a unique race. "I want to run faster," doesn't mean anything

relatively speaking, but "I want to run a four-and-a-half-minute mile," tells you a lot about what that athlete wants to achieve. The numbers measure a real speed and give you an idea of what kind of training needs to occur to get to that goal.

- *Your small goals can lead to big wins.* If you set smaller, short-term, and attainable goals, you will feel better about achieving them, and they will be minor milestones on your journey toward sports success.

- *Your goals can be slightly out of reach.* Even if you don't manage to reach your goal, you continue to push for it. Aiming high will still mean that you achieve great results. (That whole shoot for the moon saying…)

- *Make your goals fun.* That's how Katie Ledecky creates and keeps her goals–she doesn't focus so much on the end result, but on the *process* of achieving her goal. Some people might call this "enjoying the journey and not the destination." Ledecky loves her sport and is happy to be doing it, so no matter what, she's enjoying herself. This means that for her, practice doesn't seem like work. Having fun with what she's doing keeps her motivated to keep working to reach one goal and working harder to meet the next. This makes sense–after all, you *are playing a game.* Play! Figure out how to have fun as you work on your skills.

- *Successfully reaching your goals means you need to celebrate!* Before you go on to reset your goals, make sure you celebrate the one you've already achieved. Make a note of it, add it to a calendar, a journal, or post it on your favorite social media site. You did it! Congratulations! Once you enjoy your success, you can go create another goal you can achieve (Scott 2016). This–along with having fun– will keep you from burning out by stressing too much and too hard on the end results.

Using Acronym Methods of Goal Setting:

An easy way to set goals is to create an acronym; an acronym is a pronounceable word formed from the first letter of a word in a phrase or title.

Two commonly used acronyms for goal-setting use the words "goal" and "smart."

G: ("gut") A good goal matters to you; you can feel it in your gut.

O: ("objective") A good goal is objective and measurable.

A: ("achievable") A good goal is challenging, but, most of all, achievable.

L: ("learn") A good goal will help you to learn about your performance capacity.

Another word people like to use when setting goals is the word, "smart."

S: ("specific") You know exactly what your goal is.

M: ("measurable")

A: ("achievable")

R: ("realistic")

T: ("timing") You have a start and an end date.

Either one or both of these acronyms are an easy way for you to remember the characteristics of good goals so that when you set them, you know they'll work for you. (Mind Tools, n.d.)

Setting goals is not only important in sports. The ability to set goals and attain them is extremely constructive and will help you succeed in every area of life, including school, your job, your relationships, and more.

Let's walk through SMART goals using a non-sports-related example: your relationship.

Saying "I want to improve my relationship" is a goal, but it's not going to help you decide how to improve it. It's non-specific. After all, what do you mean by saying, "improve"? That could mean just about anything. A better way to approach this is by setting goals based on the things you and your partner or family member do together. Think about it. In any effective relationship, there is:

- Communication
- Problem-solving
- One-on-one time
- Paying attention to their needs and desires–and having your needs and desires met as well

With that list in mind, what can you improve using SMART goals (specific, measurable, achievable, realistic, timed)? What would a SMART goal look like for, say, communication with a family member?

- *At the end of each day, we will spend at least 15 minutes each night, listening* (remember, listening is part of communication!) *to each other as we talk about our days.* You might even set specific times and days to do this if your family has busy schedules. So, *Every other day, we will...* Some people even Facetime every night before bed, especially if they haven't been able to see each other or talk during the day.

- *Choose three things you know your partner or family member hates doing, and help them with it— or do it for them—every week. Or choose three things you can do each week on a regular basis that makes them feel appreciated. Tell them what you're doing and ask them to do the same for you; doing this is an active way to learn more about your partner and to show each other appreciation.*

The point is, performing these goals together will improve your overall communication. Each one is specific, measurable (there are time limits), achievable, realistic, and timely (Harris 2019).

EXERCISE #4: GOALS CREATE GROWTH

Before I describe this exercise, let me share a personal secret with you.

I used to not set goals. Okay, maybe that's not a giant secret, but still...it's kind of embarrassing, considering you're reading this book.

The thing is, I was afraid, convinced I'd fail. Rather, I thought that if I created a goal and wrote it down and then didn't achieve it, I'd have to stare my failure in the face and accept the fact that I was...a loser. What I failed to realize about failure (!) is that until you realize failure gives you another opportunity to excel, you won't. You'll just stay where you are with no growth, no challenges, and no motivation to become greater. Once I accepted that idea, I stopped seeing them as an obstacle I could be stopped by and started to see that goals created an opportunity for growth.

This exercise will once again require some writing. But I think you'll find it useful! If you'd rather use a separate piece of paper or your computer to complete this exercise, you can. In fact, I recommend it–and taping your finished goal chart to your bedroom wall or in your locker so you can see it several times a day.

You don't have to use a box for each, but it will make each part of your exercise stand out on its own. Also, I recommend writing the first part in pencil (so you can erase if you need to) and also recommend green ink (for "go", of course) or red in the last question (for "stop") as you create your thought answer.

1- Determine what goal you want to accomplish.

Write "What I Want to Accomplish" in this box in pencil, and then write your answer underneath it (in the same box) in green ink:

```



```

2-Determine why you want to accomplish this goal.

In the box, write: "Why I Want to Accomplish (insert your goal) in pencil, and then write your answer underneath it–again, in green ink, in the same box.

```



```

3-How will you achieve your goal?

In the box, write: "What I Need to Do to Achieve This Goal" in pencil, and then write your answer underneath it, in green ink, in the same box. (You can write this as action steps to take in a list or in a sentence).

4-What Obstacles Might Stop You?

In the box, write: "What Can Stand in My Way" in pencil, and then write your list of obstacles in red ink. You might even go further and think of ways to overcome these obstacles (which you'd write in green).

(Kuhn 2020)

Now that you've created some goals, let's discuss how you can use visualization to achieve them. Read on.

5

VISUALIZATION: THE SINGLE BEST TOOL FOR GOAL SETTING

"Set your goals high, and don't stop til you get there."

— BO JACKSON, ALL STAR NFL AND MLB

PLAYER

Now that we've got a good handle on goal-setting, let's talk about using visualization to help you achieve your goals. There's no doubt, especially in sports, that whenever you have goals to reach, visualization is the tool that will get you there. The reason for this is that while effective goal-setting will give you all the advantages we discussed in the last chapter, psychologists, coaches, and athletes alike all know that visualizing those goals as you move toward them keeps you grounded and—most importantly—motivated. Combining visualization with goal setting gives you more confidence and more sense of control—not complete certainty, but you'll have a clear view of the road ahead.

In chapter three, we discussed visualization and how anyone can do it with practice. It can't be stressed enough how you need to set aside the time—every day—to visualize if you expect to be successful at it. Just like Michael Phelps and other athletes who use it for success, you need to work at it by setting aside a time and a place for your visualization. Unfortunately, many of us become so distracted by other things going on in life—interpersonal relationships, school work, social life, social media, work, and other priorities—that we lose focus of our goals. Daily visualization sessions will help to focus our minds on those goals and keep them a priority instead of letting them slip behind the rest of the events in our lives (Brooks 2021).

While it's easy to say what we want to achieve, setting the goals by writing them down and then visualizing them will keep you motivated to make them happen. When we are distracted by life events, we frequently allow days, months, and then even years to slip away from us.

There are three things you need to consider when practicing your visualization:

1- You must visualize your skills correctly, without mistakes or bad form.
2-You must be precise in your visualization.
3-You have to repeat these visualizations frequently.

The same neural (nerve) pathways we use when we are performing a task or activity are utilized when we visualize a particular activity. What this means is—as you visualize, you're training your brain for actual performance. Mental exercise like this has been discovered to boost confidence, boost motivation, improve motor performance and increase your state of what some people call *flow*.

Flow is that feeling some athletes experience when they're performing at their best; some people call it "being in the zone." You can more easily and frequently experience flow through a combination of goal-setting and visualization. (Below, we'll discuss more about being in the state of flow.)

HOW TO USE VISUALIZATION TO ACHIEVE YOUR GOALS

As discussed in the previous sections, the more specific you are in your visualization, the better it will work. You need to have specific, measurable goals, and you need to utilize all of your five senses in your visualization. Something else to consider is what emotions you'll experience as you achieve your desired outcome. Will you feel joy? Pride? Elation? A combination of all three? Or something else? As you visualize your success, let yourself feel that emotion. The more you can feel what it'll be like to accomplish the goal, the more you'll believe it can be attained. And the more likely you'll be to act to achieve it.

Some sports psychologists recommend writing about what you need to visualize prior to actually doing it. The reason for this is that it will help you to stay focused and use your visualization time constructively. One thing to note is that when you write things down, it will activate different parts of your brain. This will allow you to attack your visualization from additional angles, adding details and descriptions to help you "see" what you need to see in order to be successful. You might even choose to include those details step-by-step in a list, breaking down the entire process in sequence until you can feel it physically and emotionally as you perform it in your mind.

Meditation as a Visualization Method

Meditation is a type or method of what is often called *mindfulness*. Like visualization, it involves sitting in a quiet place and often involves mentally focusing on a word or phrase purposefully or "mindfully." Like visualization, it is often used to help with anxiety or stress and helps people quiet their minds through disciplined concentration.

The following steps are what's known as a "guided" visualization or meditation, meaning it tells you exactly what to imagine, step by step (Thorp 2016).

1- Choose a specific goal using the acronyms discussed in chapter four (G.O.A.L. or S.M.A.R.T.). Make sure it's meaningful for you so that you'll have a great level of accomplishment once it's achieved.

2- Imagine the best possible outcome for this. What will achieving this goal produce? What difference will it make in your life?

3- Imagine your life after achieving your goal. As we've discussed, it doesn't matter if you imagine this from the inside out (from your point of view) or from the outside as a spectator; what does matter is utilizing all your senses.

4- Now, imagine that you're floating into the air above where you are now. Take your mental image (you, achieving your performance goal). Take a deep breath and as you do, use it to give energy to your visualization by imagining your breath filling it with positivity. Do this five times.

5- Next, imagine floating into your future with your performance goal and dropping it, along with your success, into your life by the date and time you've set for this goal.

6- Visualize the process you've gone through to make this success possible.

7- Once you feel you've completed your goal thoroughly and successfully, come back to now. With your eyes still closed, think about what action steps you will need to take to move you closer to your goal.

8- Take a few deep breaths before opening your eyes; once you do, I suggest you write your list of steps down and journal about your experience.

9- Every day, continue to visualize and practice the skills necessary to move you closer to your goal.

10- Remember, if you can see it, you can believe it, and, more importantly, you can make it happen! Just setting goals can help you to determine what you need to do to achieve the success you desire but visualization will help move you toward them, especially if you start with the end in mind.

Professional Athletes Who Find Success Through Meditation :

Let's discuss a few highly successful athletes who are at the top of their games and who credit meditation as part of their performance success (Williams 2019).

- **Stephen Curry:** This NBA star uses meditation and visualization to stay mindful in his moments on the floor. Meditation helps to calm his mind and keep him thinking one step ahead of his opponents so he can be one of the greatest players of all time, not only physically, but mentally.
- **Derek Jeter:** Twenty-year Yankee shortstop Derek Jeter was on 5 World Series winning teams and was selected for the All Stars fourteen times. During his years in the MLB, he meditated for about an hour every day and believes it not only helped him to be a better athlete but a better person overall.

- **Carli Lloyd:** Two-time gold medalist and two-time FIFA Women's World Cup Champion soccer player considered meditation as important to her success as conditioning and skill practice. She has been quoted as saying, "I've basically visualised so many different things on the field, making these big plays, scoring goals." She used meditation to help her stay focused and block distractions.

- **Ben Simmons:** Ben has said that using meditation and visualization ("mental health training") has taught him to be mindful in the moment and focused on the present. This has helped him to block out distractions during NBA games and not sweat things outside of his control. Instead, he hones his attention in on the things he *can* control so he can play his best.

- **Lebron James:** LA Laker James has said that meditation is responsible for his basketball success. In fact, he's even used time-outs to meditate and get himself refocused for on-court success. As a result, "King James" is considered to be one of the greatest NBA players of all time.

- **The Seattle Seahawks:** The 2014 Super Bowl Winning team was introduced to meditation by head coach, Pete Carroll. He hired a sports psychologist to work with all the Seahawks during that year, and he credited meditation with helping them to perform their best and win.

CHAPTER EXERCISE #5: PUTTING IT TOGETHER

In this exercise, you're going to use the techniques we've been discussing for visualization and the information about goal-setting from chapter four.

Simply pick a goal you've already decided on using exercise #4, or decide on a different one using the G.O.A.L. and/or S.M.A.R.T. methods. Then visualize yourself achieving that goal using any visualization methods already discussed, especially those from chapter three. Don't forget to journal the exercise for future reference!

In the next chapter, we're going to discuss using the power of mental imagery to increase your confidence and improve your performance so you can make the clutch plays you've always wanted to.

6

BUILDING CONFIDENCE FOR SPORTS PERFORMANCE THROUGH VISUALIZATION

"One important key to success is self-confidence. An important key to self-confidence is preparation."

— *TENNIS LEGEND, ARTHUR ASHE*

Visualization doesn't just work on removing your anxiety and improving your game. It can also help you build your confidence. Confidence is something we use in daily life, not just in sports. And there are visualization exercises to help you experience better levels of confidence.

SELF-CONFIDENCE AND SPORTS

Real self-confidence in sports is the belief that you can create and execute a game plan, perform a specific maneuver, and do what is necessary to win. It's also about trusting yourself and your skills. When you are confident in yourself, you have a positive attitude and realistic expectations of your abilities. As a result, you're willing to take risks because you believe in your skills and in your training. When you feel confident in your athleticism, you're able to turn your potential into performance success, but when you feel unsure or anxious about your abilities, the smallest setback or perceived failure can negatively affect your performance (Kuloor and Kumar 2021.).

Psychologists have determined there are three types of confidence.

1- Optimal self-confidence. This means the athlete is positive they'll achieve their goals. Every athlete needs to have optimal self-confidence if they're going to be at peak performance. (So if you want to be clutch, you need to be confident in yourself and your skills.)

2- Lack of confidence. Obviously, this self-doubt is almost a guarantee that you'll fail. You will be anxious, unable to concentrate, and indecisive, especially in a clutch situation.

3- **Overconfidence**. We all know athletes like this. They swagger, they brag, but when it's time to get clutch, they fail. Mostly this is because they rely on pumping themselves up to be great without putting in the work to make this a reality. They don't work on their skills, make bad judgment calls, and let down their team members who may have been believing the over-confident athlete's claims of their prowess.

A lot of people see football great, Tom Brady, as arrogant. (Or, overconfident.) But when you look into his story, you learn that he was simply confident. He had to be—no one else was. His skills weren't great, his body was "wrong," he didn't have sufficient strength for an NFL quarterback, and some people have even said that "he runs funny." But here's a story about how he met his boss, owner Rob Kraft, when first drafted by the Pats in 2000. He walked up to his billionaire boss and said, "I'm Tom Brady."

Kraft answered, "I know who you are. You're our 6th round draft pick."

In epic Brady-fashion, he looked Kraft in the eyes and said, "That's right. And I'm the best decision this organization has ever made (Schleien 2021)."

Arrogance, yes, maybe. Confidence—definitely! He hadn't even had the opportunity to prove himself on the field, and if Drew Bledsoe hadn't gotten injured, he might never have had the chance. But he didn't give up on himself; instead, he believed in himself.

He couldn't predict that he'd win more Super Bowls than any other quarterback in NFL history, or be the recipient of multiple MVPs. He didn't know he'd still be playing football–and winning!--even when most quarterbacks are retired. But he didn't give up on himself. Instead, *he put in the work to make himself great*. He didn't rely on his skills–because it was "obvious" to any scouts or teams watching him prior to the draft that he didn't have the skills necessary to make it in the league.

It's interesting to point out that while Brady is still playing at the time of this writing in 2022, the quarterback drafted in the first round (in 2000), Chad Pennington, *never* won a Super Bowl, though he did lead his team to two playoff wins. (Let's give credit where credit is due.) According to the "experts," he was the one to beat. And Brady was a nobody-nothing player who wasn't expected to do much of anything.

The thing is–they couldn't measure his confidence.

Self-confidence is an important predictor of success. But not everyone has Tom Brady-like self-belief. What can you do if you're not confident in yourself and your athletic abilities?

Six Ways to Build Your Confidence

1- Realize You're a Work in Progress.

What this means is—you're not "done." In fact, you're not done until you don't—or can't—try anymore. As long as you keep playing, practicing, and working on your skills, there's hope for improvement. So what if you feel like you're no good today? Don't focus on the last play—it's done. Focus on the next play, and the play after that and know that you can become the athlete you envision yourself to be, but the only way to do that is to never give up.

2-Practice, practice, and then–practice some more!

Nothing builds confidence like sharply-tuned skills and knowing you can switch them on at will. Don't stop practicing, even when you think you can't practice anymore. No one's ever practiced so much that their skills declined; they only got better and better. After all, look at Tom Brady; he just kept practicing.

3-Have patience with yourself.

You're not going to be perfect right out of the gate. In fact, you might have to accept that sometimes, you're going to suck! But in your mind you need to keep the idea that there is no failure. Instead, every poor performance is another opportunity to learn and grow–and to attain a higher level of excellence in the future. Realize that the greatest athletes are made, not born; they create their greatness through hard work over a sustained period of time. That takes patience. And persistence.

4-Don't Give Up.

See above. Be persistent! Keep trying. Keep practicing. Tell yourself that you can do it–and believe it! Surfer great, Laird Hamilton, puts it this way: "Make sure your worst enemy doesn't live between your own two ears." In other words, you can talk yourself right into giving up because you don't have self-confidence. If you hear yourself putting yourself down–don't listen! Fight back by working harder to be as clutch as you *know* you can be.

5-Focus on Being the Best You Can Be.

Of course, when you play a sport, the most obvious goal is to win. But that shouldn't be the only goal, or even the most important. As an athlete, your most important goal should be–always–doing your best. And yes, it sucks if you or your team loses. You know, sometimes one team really is better than another; that's just another truth about sporting events. You can't change that. But what you can do is focus on being the best you can be. The thing is–if you do your best and continue to do your best in every game situation–then you can be confident that you didn't lose for lack of effort.

6- Visualize Yourself As Confident.

The good news is–even if you have no self-confidence–you can train yourself to be confident by using visualization.

How to Use Visualization to Increase Your Confidence

By using these techniques, not only can you increase your self-esteem and your confidence in your athleticism, but also in your everyday life.

Here are four ways to visualize yourself into being self-confident:

1-Anchoring It In.

- Get into your visualization place and space, where it's quiet and you're comfortable.
- Think of a time when you felt extremely confident.
- Remember the feelings you had at that moment; the elation, the pride, the sense of accomplishment. Bring back every detail that you can.
- Once you're "there", press the tip of your right index finger against the top of your thumb.

You'll want to do this more than once; maybe a few times. The reason? Doing this is called "anchoring"; what it does is create a sense-memory connection. Ultimately, what you want is that whenever you repeat that action of pressing your index finger to the top of your thumb, you automatically bring back those feelings and the confidence you had.

2-Mentally Rehearsing Yourself Confident:

- If you're going to be in a situation where you need confidence, once again, get into your visualization place and space.
- Close your eyes, and breathe deeply five times.
- Begin to imagine the situation. As you would with any visualization, get as detailed as you can. But in this scenario, you include the detail of you being confident. If you've already established the ability to use anchoring as described above, try it here to bring back those good feelings. Repeat as often as you desire up until that event.

3-Put on Your Confidence Shoes.

Have you ever heard the saying, "Put yourself in the other person's shoes"? Well, this is similar. What you want to do here is visualize yourself in the place of one of the most confident persons you may know.

- In your visualization, notice how they move, stand, walk, talk; are they loud or soft? Do they make direct eye contact? How do they greet people? How do you know they are confident?
- Once you've got them visualized, step into their shoes. In their shoes, you're going to be the same way they are—confident. In your visualization, notice how people respond to you. They know you are confident too.
- Repeat this exercise as often as you feel a need to boost your confidence. There's another saying: "Fake it till you make it"--here, you're faking it, but your mind doesn't know that the situation isn't real. You will be training yourself to be the confident person you wish to be!

4-Boost Your Self-Esteem Through Self-Suggestion:

Repetition is powerful. Think of a jingle for a product that you hear often. It only plays on your television or computer or whatever for about ten seconds at a time. But marketers run it often. Pretty soon, you can't even think of one of the words in the jingle without hearing the entire thing playing in your head. It's stuck there, annoying and unhelpful—until you need that product.

And then–probably–it will be the company that you go to.

This suggestion is a lot like that. You need to put words in your head, and they need to get stuck on repeat so that you automatically hear them when you need them (and even when you don't). Remember how we discussed meditation in the last chapter? I mentioned that some people who meditate focus on a word or phrase during their meditation or visualization. For this exercise, you will too. Focus on things like:

- "I am confident."
- "I believe in myself."
- "I am a great athlete."
- "I know I can do (whatever it is that you need or want to achieve)."
- "I am clutch."

Find a phrase that works for you, and make it part of your thoughts. Pretty soon, it will transform your thoughts about yourself and shape you into the self-confident person and athlete you want to be.

5-Talk to Yourself as You Would a Friend.

For some reason, most of us talk to ourselves nega-tively, saying things we'd never say to a friend. Maybe we think we're being honest when we call ourselves names or point out negative things, but the fact is we're only hurting ourselves. When performing these mental exercises, be sure to speak kindly and positively to yourself, just like you would to a friend. Those kind words have a greater effect than negative ones (Hutchison 2018)!

Being Clutch So Far: A Quick Recap

Up to this point, we've discussed using visualization to help you improve your athletic skills and performance, and how to set and achieve your goals using visualization. We touched on using visualization to improve your self-esteem and your self-confidence. Let's do a quick review of some of the guidelines for visualization before we move on.

When you visualize, you should always begin by being in your quiet, calm place. Soccer legend Pelé was known to lie on a bench with a towel over his head before each game so he could mentally rehearse his skills and envision different game scenarios without distraction; if you need to create your own space and place with a towel or similar item, do it (Simpson 2017). Don't worry about what your teammates might think; once they begin to see the results of your visualizations, they'll probably soon be under towels of their own.

To begin, focus on your breathing. This will direct your attention inward and onto relaxation. It will help you to slow down your body and your thoughts so that you can begin to make your mental imagery more detailed and intense. In turn, it will be more effective. Remember, you'll want to use all of your senses and put yourself in that imagery emotionally as well as physically. By doing this, your mind will believe it's real and actually happening, bringing the best benefits of the exercise to you.

When visualizing for sports performance, if it's better and easier for you to use the perspective of a coach or a spectator, that's the way you should do it. But if you're meditating and visualizing for confidence, it's suggested you do so from the inside looking out (First person). Experiencing your internal confidence and your other positive emotions is the way to etch that self-esteem into your neural pathways.

One other thing: when you're visualizing for performance, you'll be imagining yourself at a specific event, race, or game. But when visualizing for confidence, see the confident You in the present, not as something that will happen someday or in the future. Let you have self-confidence *now*.

Try different techniques/methods/or approaches and discover what works the best for you. You may find that some methods are more effective than others, or that only one works but it works perfectly, or that all techniques are effective for you in different instances.

SOME OTHER WAYS TO USE VISUALIZATION

Visualization is a powerful tool to use for other emotions or situations; it's worthwhile to touch on those things here. You may find that some of these may resonate with you as something you need to use, whether in sports or in other areas of your life.

1- Visualization to overcome fear (of failure):

Identify the situation making you fearful. What are you afraid of? (Be specific.)

Realize that there are things that you truly need to be afraid of, and things that you only think you need to be afraid of–the *what ifs.*

As I've said, the brain doesn't know what is real and what you are imagining. While this is great for positive visualization, it's also terrible when it comes to made-up scenarios where you ask, "What if…(I fail)?" When you imagine yourself failing, you will experience all the negative emotions that you'd feel at that moment, just as if it's truly happening to you. You need to reframe the fear and recreate the scenario through visualization.

One way to do this is to visualize the situation. Let's say–because it's a common fear, and one I've experienced–that you have to speak in front of a roomful of people. Visualize yourself on stage, behind (or maybe not) a podium or desk.

Ask yourself–what's the worst that can happen? You lose your place in your speech...you drop your notes and don't know what to say...everyone stops listening to you...a dinosaur suddenly crashes through the back of the room and–

Oh? You're not worried about the dinosaur? Why not? Because it's not real. And that's true of the entire thought process. You're imagining this, making it up, and frightening yourself into inactivity. But remember–you are in control here. You are the one giving the speech in this visualization. You stand straight and tall. You are confident! You are prepared, and you know your material so well, even if you do drop your notes, it doesn't matter. You don't need them! Everyone is listening to you. They are nodding and smiling because what you're saying resonates with them. At the end, they applaud.

Instead of soaking your brain with the hormones that it secretes during fight, flight or freeze situations (and fearful ones, real or imagined)- let it bathe in the "happy hormones" it secretes when you're successful, like Dopamine and Endorphins (Raypole 2019).

2- Visualizing to Overcome Procrastination:

Procrastination ties into fear. When people are afraid of something (or doing something)--or maybe just don't want to do something (like take a test), they tend to delay doing whatever it is they need to do. The good news is--you can visualize yourself out of procrastinating into successful completion of that task!

I can give you an example. Most athletes go to the gym, especially in their off-season, to stay in shape and healthy. But going to the gym is a chore; you might not feel like going, especially after being at school or work, or both, all day. It's easier to procrastinate. But you can use visualization to motivate yourself to go, and even better, to have a successful workout.

Begin by getting into your visualization space and place, and get ready to visualize. This is a good place to explain that it actually helps if you break the task into smaller steps. So, for example, you might begin by visualizing yourself packing whatever you might need to take to the gym, like your water and a towel.

Or maybe you'll visualize yourself doing a particular exercise. Let's use the treadmill as an example. You get onto the machine and start it slowly, walking as a warm-up. Feel your muscles tingling and your heart beginning to beat faster, feel the blood flowing through your limbs, and the exhilaration that occurs as the endorphins (the "feel good hormones") are released by your brain. You increase the speed on the machine; the belt beneath your feel whirrs and your feel make a rhythmic pounding sound as you begin to run...continue your run, increasing your speed and your inclines until you've run as far or as long as you need to, then open your eyes.

By this exercise, I'm motivated to approach the task I've been avoiding–running on the treadmill–because *I've already experienced the success of it.* I realize that it's not impossible–it's simply something I don't especially want to do. But that doesn't mean I *can't* do it. I can, and I do, because I've seen it happen (in my visualization). And I visualize how good I'll physically feel after completing my workout. Maybe even more importantly, I try to capture that completion mental feeling, that feeling that I made progress towards my goal. Because if you think about why you started in the first place, you're much more likely to become remotivated.

3- Visualization for overcoming self-doubt:

Self-doubt is another thing motivated by fear of failure. Like low self-esteem or lack of confidence, it's a negative opinion you hold of yourself, and it can cause you to believe you are unable to succeed in a situation. In a way, having self-doubt is the opposite of having confidence. But by now, you know you are able to visualize yourself into having confidence.

One suggested visualization is called, "The Spotlight of Excellence" (Hamilton 2017). What it does is connect you to a mental place you have had in the past when you've successfully performed in your sport.

Visualize yourself on the field or in an arena. A huge spotlight is centered on the ground or floor in front of you; now, think back to that situation of peak performance, when everything seemed to work just right, and you didn't worry or have any anxiety about what you needed to do. Everything flowed without any effort.

Now, visualize yourself from the outside, standing outside that circle of light, looking into the circle. In that circle, you see yourself–excelling at your sport. You can hear, taste, smell, feel everything from that moment when you achieved excellence.

Step into the spotlight and slip into that image of you so that you are experiencing excellence again in real-time. Notice what you are feeling and seeing; whenever you begin to doubt yourself, bring yourself into that spotlight of excellence again and remember the experience.

More Exercises to Restore Your Self-Confidence

Exercise 1: This written exercise can help provide stability to your confidence by using visualization to bring confidence to situations where you may feel fear or self-doubt.

Get your pen or pencil ready, and divide your page into two columns. (You can use your visualization journal or notebook if you've created one so that you can refer to this list again–or change it up–later.)

- At the top of the first column, write: *High-confidence Situations*; at the top of the second column, write: *Low-confidence Situations*.
- In the first column, list all of the sports-related situations or events that have in the past or will in the future bring you confidence.
- In the second column, list all of the situations or events that you know can erode or diminish your self-confidence.
- Using this list, you can tap into the positive emotions and sensations from the high-confidence column and visualize them into the situations and events in the low-confidence column, taking the negative feelings and fears away.

Exercise 2: This is another written exercise, and it uses positive self-talk.

Basically, you will use it to affirm to yourself that you have the skills, abilities, attitudes, and everything you need to be successful at your sport. What you will do is write positive statements you can repeat to yourself as necessary. You can use this in conjunction with the self-suggestion exercise discussed above; a combination of writing and visualizing can be even more powerful because one reinforces the positive message of the other.

- Create a list of four to five affirmations like, "I am strong," "I am powerful," "I am clutch," etc.
- Read this list every night before you go to bed and every morning when you wake up.
- Repeatedly exposing yourself to these statements–especially when your mind is half-awake–embeds them into your subconscious mind. Eventually, they will become strong beliefs that will have a powerful influence on your performance (Hamilton 2017).

Exercise 3: Research has discovered that being involved with the success of teammates or others can boost your confidence (Hamilton 2017).

What this means is–if you help someone learn or better their sports skills, then you will feel a sense of confidence and accomplishment that you can use in your own sports-related performance.

I experienced this phenomenon myself on a high school skiing trip. Even though I wasn't a great skier, or even a good one (I fell down at least once, if not more, every run), I enjoyed the sport and was always ready to strap on my boards and go whether I had friends with me or not.

During this one trip, I was cautiously and carefully heading down an intermediate slope (telling myself not to fall the whole time and falling anyway) when I came across a girl from the trip. "Kelly" was in a steep and icy place where she couldn't safely take off her skis and walk to the bottom of the hill (which, to be honest, wasn't even visible from where we were.) A brand-new skier, she'd naively followed her more advanced "friends" onto an intermediate-level slope and then–when she couldn't keep up with them–found herself abandoned. She was cold, crying, trembling, and absolutely terrified.

Of course, I couldn't leave her there. I gave her an only slightly squashed fun-sized candy bar for a quick boost of energy *and* because chocolate makes *everything* better; it took a little time, but once I'd gotten her to laugh and relax, I was able to convince her that standing still wouldn't get her to the lodge and that she needed to ski the rest of the way down.

Once she began to relax and trust herself, and me, *and the mountain*, skiing came more easily, and she fell less. Eventually–about an hour later–we made it to the end of the run. I helped her get her skis off, and after she thanked me profusely, she went to the lodge to warm up. I wasn't ready to quit yet, so I got back in line for the ski lift; as I waited for my chair, I suddenly realized–during that whole time I was helping Kelly, I hadn't fallen at all.

In fact, I'd skied the entire rest of the run *backward and facing uphill*. I'd been so focused on helping her finish her run safely and teaching her the skills that she needed to get off the ski slope (and maybe have a little fun in the process) that I'd completely forgotten how much I was convinced that I sucked at skiing.

I'd like to be able to say that after this experience, I discovered I was a world-class skier, but I can't. What I can say, however, is that my confidence in my abilities grew tenfold. I stopped telling myself (and everyone else) that I wasn't any good at skiing. After that, I was able to just be in the moment and enjoy myself–which is ultimately what sports should be about.

With this story in mind, consider who you know–a friend, a teammate, or just someone you see struggling with a specific sport skill that you know you can help them with, and go help them. To be honest, while it seems like it's just a nice thing to do, when you help someone learn a skill, you're also teaching it to yourself.

Even if you already understand how to do it, when you're showing it to someone else, you need to break it down into its basic components and–usually–demonstrate them. This tends to make your technique much better and cleaner because they need to be able to see what you're doing and understand how it works.

Ultimately, helping someone helps you. (And makes you feel good, too.)

More Athletes Who Have Confidence

There are so many athletes who have learned or earned (or both) very high levels of confidence, but the most confident also tend to be the most elite. All you need to do is an internet search on "most confident elite athletes" and dozens of names will pop up.

One of the most confident athletes whose name will come up is tennis player, Serena Williams. You can see it whenever she steps on the court. Williams plays with a ferocious passion and emotion that she's not afraid to show to the world.

Another confident player is Lionel (Leo) Messi. At 5'7", he doesn't seem to be the kind of guy to stand up to and compete against much more athletic-appearing soccer players, but he's quick, he's elite, and he is one of the best and most well-known in the world.

Retired track and field star, Usain Bolt, is considered to be one of the fastest people in the world. He holds eight Olympic gold medals and is the only sprinter to win Olympic 100-meter and 200-meter titles at three consecutive Olympics. You know he's confident because he famously said, "I told you all I was going to be number one, and I did just that" to the press.

Now *that's* confidence!

CHAPTER EXERCISE #6: MAKE CONFIDENCE YOUR OWN

Go back to the "More Exercises to Restore Your Self-Confidence" section and read exercises 1 and 2. Using the list from exercise 1 so you know what needs you have, create a list of 4 to 5 affirmations. For 21 days, every morning on waking up and every night before going to sleep, repeat those affirmations to yourself. Why 21 days? Because that's how long it takes for something to become a habit, and once you've made repeating those affirmations a habit, they will become a part of you–and your self-confidence!

All right. Now, it's time to consider another significant aspect of sporting excellence. All the physical conditioning, skills practice, and mental imagery you've spent time on will fail you when you least expect it if you overlook one key aspect of sports performance—nutrition. Nutrition is more related to visualization in sports than you may well have previously thought.

Read on to learn more in the next chapter.

7

SPORTS NUTRITION, AND HOW IT'S CRUCIAL TO PHYSICAL AND MENTAL PERFORMANCE FOR YOUNG ATHLETES

"The best abs exercise is 5 sets of Stop Eating So Much Crap."

— *FITNESS COACH LAZAR ANGELOV*

W hen it comes to sports performance, particularly among young athletes, a major factor that often gets overlooked is the importance of having a good diet. What you eat influences your body not only physically but also mentally—including the ability to make visualization work the way it's meant to. (Example: No amount of visualizing will help you make your first-ever basketball dunk in today's morning game if you've been skipping breakfast and eating nothing but chocolate bars for lunch the entire week!)

After mental and physical training, one more aspect that every elite athlete needs to be aware of is nutrition. Without good nutrition, we deprive our bodies of much-needed fuel, leaving them dehydrated, fatigued, and unable to optimally recover after exercise. This chapter discusses nutrition, including how it affects mental performance in sports.

We will also discuss the habits of some professional athletes who are famous for their bad nutrition. While the media and the fans enjoy and even celebrate their favorite sports hero's food habits, in some cases (like Dwayne Howard's), those athletes took themselves out of the game entirely because their poor diets and food choices catastrophically affected their health.

WHAT IS SPORTS NUTRITION?

Sports nutrition is about providing individual athletes with the ideal amounts and combinations of foods to help them achieve their best performance. Proper nutrition also helps the body recover more quickly from injuries and tissue rebuilding after workouts.

Sports nutritionists work to determine what foods and fluids the athlete requires to stay well-hydrated and properly fueled to function at their peak levels. It is unique to each person and is planned according to individual goals. It can also vary based on the amount of energy to be expelled at game time or during a sporting event and can be different every day (Leal 2018).

The Basics of Sports Nutrition

Foods are broken into different categories; all of them play a specific role in nutrition. You probably know about them because it's hard to escape learning and hearing about them pretty much everywhere.

But just in case, let's go over them.

Carbohydrates

The human body uses carbohydrates (carbs) for the majority of its energy. Carbs are considered either simple or complex, depending on how they're created or made and how the body breaks them down into fuel.

- Simple carbohydrates-these are the sugars that occur in foods like fruits, vegetables, and milk.
- Complex carbs occur in whole grain breads, most vegetables, oats, and potatoes.

Both simple and complex carbohydrates are broken down in the digestive system to form glucose–or sugar–to supply energy to your cells, muscles, and organs.

Proteins

The body uses protein in muscle growth and recovery, but it's important to every cell the body contains. Made up of amino acid chains, protein is considered either complete or incomplete; essential amino acids are necessary to the body's health, and because the body can't produce them, they have to come from the foods we eat.

- Complete proteins have all the amino acids the body requires and comes from animal sources like meat, fish, poultry, and milk.
- Incomplete proteins usually lack one or more of the essential amino acids; these are usually proteins from plant sources.

Fats

The word *fat* has a bad reputation, but as a food source, fats are vital. There are two types of fats:

- Unsaturated fats are considered "the healthy fat"; they come from plant sources like olives and nuts. They provide energy and help with body health and development, such as

maintaining cell membranes and protecting our organs.
- Saturated fats come from dairy products and red meat and may be less healthy.

Carbohydrates and/or fats are used as the body's main sources of energy. It depends on the amount of exercise and its intensity; not consuming enough food can negatively affect your athleticism and performance.

Many professional athletes go to sports nutritionists to help them determine what types of these three foods and in what percentage they need them in order to fuel their sports performance. The amounts vary from person to person; the intensity of their workouts will also affect how much food is required.

As a young athlete, especially one who is currently in their adolescence, when the body undergoes massive changes in growth and hormones, nutrition is especially important. You want to be sure you're giving yourself enough fuel not only to perform to your best, but to grow well too.

Nutritionists recommend at least five additional–or more!--pieces of fruit and vegetables a day. You can use green drinks and smoothies as part of your nutrition to get these into your body without having to add them to your meals.

THE IMPORTANCE OF HYDRATION IN SPORTS PERFORMANCE

I think every athlete is aware of how important it is to have water available when you're practicing or playing. How many times have you heard a trainer, coach, teacher, or parent say, "Where's your water? Do you have your water? Take a water break! Drink your water!" And I think all of us know about the hard-to-miss bright-orange vats of sports drinks on the side-lines at the benches of most professional games and smaller jugs in varsity games. So we all understand that hydration is important.

You may not be aware of the reasons why. The thing is, our bodies are composed of about 60 % of water; it's necessary for almost every bodily function. But our bodies cannot make their own water and they can't store it either. Because you eliminate water from your body through sweat (and urination, but not during game time, of course), you must replace the fluid you lose or suffer dire consequences, including:

- Hypohydration (dehydration)
- Hypovolemia (decreased plasma/blood volume)
- Hyponatremia (low blood sodium levels/water intoxication)

Any one of these conditions can result in hospitalization and even death. With that in mind, it's no wonder the adults in your life are constantly hounding you to stay hydrated.

It's recommended that everyone should drink at least 64 ounces of water per day and that athletes drink even more. When you are actively playing or practicing, you should drink before, during, and after. In hot weather, especially, you should try to replace the amount of water you lose through perspiration by drinking extra fluid.

Some people include sports drinks as part of their hydration routine. It's not a bad practice to have, especially in warmer weather. Look for sports drinks made up of 6% to 10% carbohydrates and read the label to be sure your drink of choice is diluted with approximately 50% water (Alaia 2014).

Keep in mind that once you feel thirsty, it's too late; you've already lost about 2% of your body weight in fluid. That's enough to hurt your performance. Also, if you drink until your thirst is just quenched, you will only get about half the amount of water or fluid that your body needs. To avoid either of these scenarios, it's best to hydrate as often as you can and not be running with a belly sloshing full of water (which can cause its own issues).

Here are some hydration tips:

- Drink small amounts of water frequently rather than gulping large amounts every once in a while.
- Try to drink cooled beverages to lower your core body temperature and reduce sweating and great water loss.
- It's recommended that you weigh yourself before and after exercise to determine your fluid loss. Follow this formula to replace water: for every pound you've lost from sweating, drink 16 to 24 oz. of water.
- Check your urine. Clear urine means you are well-hydrated. Dark-colored urine means you are less hydrated; notice the color of your urine when you get up in the morning versus how it's clear or almost-clear at the end of the day when you've had many hours of hydration (Alaia 2014).

NUTRITION HELPS WITH RECOVERY

After any vigorous workout, your muscles need time to recover. Even as you're lifting weights for your health and good muscle strength and tone, you're tearing the fibers and causing mini-injuries that need to recover–

that's why experts don't recommend working the same muscle groups on subsequent days.

Nutrition can help your body recover faster and better from this—or from actual injury. Even the best of athletes can experience injuries caused by participation in their sport; it's part of the game. Knowing what to eat to help your body repair itself so you can get back in the game is important for every athlete.

Here are suggestions to help yourself recover from sports-related injury through nutrition:

1. Eat protein-rich foods: As we've discussed, protein helps build muscle tissue. When you injure yourself, the body part you can't use will atrophy—get smaller/lose muscle from lack of use. Eating more protein can help reduce muscle loss due to inactivity. Lean chicken, fish, and sometimes beef, beans, nuts, and even tofu (soy bean curd) are good choices for restorative protein; you can ask a nutritionist or your orthopedist for recommendations of how much is an appropriate amount of protein to add to your diet (Central Orthopedic Group 2018).

2. Get more vitamin C: When you have an injury, inflammation is inevitable. It's one of the things that makes it difficult to move an injured joint

or muscle and it's something that you want to reduce as much as possible. Vitamin C helps with this; when you have an injury, consuming these C-rich foods is a good idea: oranges, grapefruits, and other citrus fruits and juices; bell peppers, spinach, tomatoes, kiwis, and broccoli. Look on the internet for other vitamin-C food options.

3. Eat more fiber-full foods: When you're not able to work out due to injury, weight gain is possible. Experts recommend eating foods high in fiber to help you feel fuller faster. This includes things like broccoli, spinach, lettuce, and other veggies and fruits. Avoid junk food. (But I bet you knew that anyway.)

Other things experts recommend to aid in sports recovery include Omega 3 fatty acids, which can be found in foods like fish and nuts, and in the oils used for cooking like sunflower and even corn oil, foods rich in zinc (again, fish and nuts are good food choices), and vitamin D and calcium, which can be found in dairy products and dark leafy green vegetables like broccoli, spinach, and kale.

What You Can Do About Your Nutrition

There is a lot of good–and bad–information about nutrition on the internet. For the best information, you should speak to your doctor. They will have your weight, height, and other stats, especially if you've been seeing the same doctor since you were born. They will know your body's composition and growth rates, and probably about where you are in your maturation process toward adulthood. So they will be able to point you in the direction of the best diet for you.

Even better, they may be able to refer you to a sports nutritionist in your area who can work with you to create an individualized nutrition plan to suit your performance needs. A sports nutritionist will also be able to offer advice about supplements to advance or increase your performance and even your whole-body health.

A WORD ABOUT SUPPLEMENTS

Supplements are part of the workout world. Many athletes, coaches, and trainers tout this or that product to increase your stamina or enhance your skills, or whatever the marketing team for that particular product decides to say.

And it's true that some supplements can be helpful, especially with recovery. But as I showed you, there are actual foods that can provide the same nutrients that a man-made, lab-produced supplement can provide. The thing is—right now, as a young athlete, you're most likely in a period of growth as your body works toward physical maturity, and its needs are particular. That is why I hesitate to recommend supplements to any teen.

One very big reason for this is that supplements aren't regulated by the FDA (Harmer 2020). You really can't be sure what you are buying—or putting into your body—when you buy and take supplements. There could be many ingredients that—while not harmful to a "finished" adult body—can be detrimental to the proper growth and maturity of a younger, maturing body. Overall, the risks outweigh the benefits, especially when you compare a well-balanced diet of *real* food (where the vitamins, minerals, and nutrient content are well-known) versus something created in a laboratory and sold for a profit by some big company.

The only time young athletes should consider supplementation is when they may have specific dietary needs that may result in a diet that is not as well-rounded as their body requires. For example, if that athlete follows a vegan or vegetarian diet, or has other health conditions like allergies associated with their diet, things can be more complicated. The athlete may not be able to attain the recommended amount of nutrients like proteins (for example). In this case, however, I would definitely recommend you see a nutritionist to get recommendations for good supplements you can trust.

Below is a chart about supplements frequently used by teenaged and young adult athletes, showing potential benefits *and* side effects. Pay particular attention to anything in a bold font and to the "Additional information" column.

Popular Supplements for Teenage Athletes:

Supplement	What it is	Effects	Risks	Additional information
Protein Powder	Usually made with whey powder, soy powder, or casein powder, or vegan.	Muscle growth and post-workout recovery.	Diarrhea, nausea, bloating. May be harmful in large doses.	Eat high-protein foods instead.
Creatine	Comes from protein-rich foods like meats, fish, dairy, eggs, nuts, seeds (like pumpkin seeds), and seaweed.	Strength increased.	May cause stomach issues, including cramps and nausea. Potential for dehydration. Possibility of weight gain.	Not safe for maturing and growing teens. Consuming a diet of well-balanced foods is recommended as an alternative.
Caffeine	Stimulant produced artificially, or naturally produced by certain plants.	May reduce fatigue and temporarily increase energy and endurance.	High doses can cause trembling, sweating, and anxiety. May be toxic in large doses.	Benefits do not outweigh the negative side effects, especially in large amounts.
BCAAs	Specific amino acids that occur in protein-rich foods, including poultry, salmon, tuna, and eggs.	May improve muscle growth and assist in fat loss. Can reduce fatigue. May strengthen the immune system's health.	Unclear research results on potential effectiveness.	The consumption of high-quality protein foods is considered a better option for teenagers than use of the supplements.

Sodium Bicarbonate	Baking soda.	Reported to reduce fatigue and increase or improve performance during sporting events.	May cause stomach issues or stomach upset.	Side effects considered potentially greater than the reported benefits.
Nitrate	Also produced by the human body.	May improve performance and endurance.	Stomach issues reported.	Not recommended for maturing individuals.
Collagen	A protein also created by the body to assist in bone support and structure.	Potential to assist in reduction of healing time for injuries.	Potential for allergic reactions, as well as stomach issues.	It is recommended to consume foods with high collagen content like meat, fish, bone broth, eggs.
HMB	Also produced by our bodies, this is also found in foods like eggs, cheese, and meat.	Reported to increase muscle size and strength. Also used for recovery improvement.	Research is inconclusive as to side effects or safety.	A balanced diet of foods containing this molecule is recommended instead.
Pre-Workout	Contains multiple supplements depending on the brand.	Reported to increase strength, boost endurance and energy.	Because the ingredients vary, conclusive results are not available.	Not recommended for teens.

(Harmer 2020)

Please note this is not too be seen as advice but as information to research further and meet with a professional. Most nutritionists for young athletes recommend food first, supplements second, and only then with caution. It can't be stated enough that supplements aren't regulated; you're never sure what is going into that powder or pill you're consuming.

Good Examples of Bad Nutrition

Just as some supplements can actually be bad for you–so can some foods. Remember how I mentioned that some athletes have potentially hurt their careers with their poor nutritional habits? Here are some stories to share with you.

Dwayne Howard: This NBA player was well-known for his sweet tooth. Sports network ESPN reported that "...Howard had been scarfing down about two dozen chocolate bars' worth of sugar every single day for years, possibly as long as a decade...Skittles, Starbursts, Rolos, Snickers, Mars bars, Twizzlers, Almond Joys, Kit Kats, and [as the Lakers' nutritionist said] 'Oh, how he loved Reese's Pieces' (McDermott 2017).

In 2013, as a result of consuming so much sugar, he developed a rare nerve disorder called *dysesthesia* which caused him to feel tingling and numbness in his extremities and also made him lose motor function so he couldn't catch passes. People who followed his career said he was a good player, but never great. Many wonder if things would have been different if he'd eaten healthier and better.

Kwame Brown: Signed into the NBA right out of high school, Brown was a highly anticipated player. But he never amounted to much, recording only one double-digit scoring season during 13 in the league. It's speculated that could have been down to his diet; Brown ate Popeye's fried chicken at every meal–even breakfast!

Caron Butler: For much of his 14 years in the NBA, Butler admitted to being addicted to Mountain Dew, consuming two full liters of the soda a day. Let's break that down. According to the American Heart Association, men should consume no more than 9 teaspoonfuls, or 36 grams, of sugar a day; a two-liter bottle of Mountain Dew contains 276 grams, or a whopping 55.2 teaspoons of sugar! Clearly, when it comes time to "Do the Dew", just don't.

Vince Young: Titans QB reportedly spent $5,000 *a week* at The Cheesecake Factory during his time on the team. As if that's not bad enough, the restaurant has been called one of the unhealthiest eateries in the United States (Picchi 2014). While this may or may not have affected his game performance, it certainly wasn't any good for his wallet.

Fortunately, you're reading this book before you make the pros, so you can start now to make better food choices to build your body into an athletic powerhouse for clutch success.

EXERCISE #7: A SAMPLE DAY'S DIET FOR THE TEENAGE ATHLETE

Review the sample day's diet plan below; notice how the meals are proportioned between good carbs, proteins, and fats. Also, look at the portion sizes. Give it a try for a day—or two—and don't be afraid to do some research on some meal preparations of your own. Also, it's okay to combine snacks and meals if you need to for the sake of convenience.

Ultimately, you want to be sure to get the right amount of calories in by the end of each day. Your goal here (unless recommended by your doctor, coach, or trainer) is not to lose weight but to be strong and healthy. In some cases, you might even be trying to gain weight! (Just do it healthfully and not by ingesting processed, nutrient-lacking foods that give you no benefits.)

Try to eat well for a few weeks and track how you feel physically and emotionally. Keep a particular eye on if your performance improves (Pritchard 2021).

(Wake-up)

- Drink 16oz. of water

Breakfast

- One cup of Greek yogurt (Oikos Pro is one of my favorites)
- Blueberries, raspberries, 1 tsp. honey, and low-sugar granola.

Mid-morning snack

- One sliced apple
- Two tablespoons of peanut butter (or use the brand PB2, it's a great alternative)

Lunch

- Burrito style bowl with chicken or steak
- White or brown rice
- Peppers
- Black or pinto beans
- Avocado
- Salsa

Pre-practice

- A scoop of whey protein powder in almond milk or water
- Banana or fruit of choice

Dinner

- Six to eight ounces of lean meat like fish or chicken
- One to two handfuls of sweet potato fries (baked or cooked in an air-fryer)
- Asparagus or other dark green vegetable

Pre-bedtime/Wind-Down Time Snack

- Popcorn
- Halo Top (or similar brand) ice cream

Summing It Up

Up to this point, we've discussed ways to get clutch and *be* clutch, ending here with eating for your best performance ever (eating clutch?). At any rate, we're at fourth and goal, rounding third, in the paint, in front of the net, match-point, in the homestretch–and whatever other sports terms you can come up with that say we're ready to cross the line and win. All we need to do is put everything we've learned together. So we're heading into our last chapter to discover how you can get the most of everything that visualization has to offer by learning how to incorporate it into your daily habits. Read on.

8

BEING CLUTCH BY MAKING VISUALIZATION YOUR CORE HABIT AS AN ATHLETE

"Watch your actions, they become your habits. Watch your habits, they become your character."

— *FOOTBALL COACH, VINCE LOMBARDI (CONSIDERED GREATEST COACH OF ALL TIME)*

The final ingredient you need to become clutch is habit. Building good habits will make it easier for you to work on your goals because once you've gained momentum, it will take less effort to push yourself harder. Let's be honest–your coach, your trainers, your teachers, your parents, and even I can give you the best advice in the world, but improvement rests on your shoulders. The way to improve–your success!-- lies in your habits.

Bear in mind, not all habits are good habits. But bad habits can negatively impact your life in a big way. All you need to do is consider the pros discussed in the last chapter, who had bad eating habits that didn't bring them good results.

Good habits, however, have the potential to launch us to our best potential and great success. It can be tough to build good habits, especially when you are starting on long-term ones. But there are ways you can use to establish good habits and break bad ones.

WHAT ARE HABITS AND WHAT DO THEY HAVE TO DO WITH SPORTS PERFORMANCE?

Habits are defined as actions we do automatically that help us to get through the day, like brushing our teeth, taking a shower, getting dressed; they're things we often do without needing to think about them. Some people call habits *rituals.* (Remember when we discussed rituals in chapter two, where we said a ritual is a ceremony or action performed in a customary way.)

Psychologists have broken habits into three categories. The first category has the habits we perform without even noticing them. For example, kicking our shoes off by the door as soon as we get in the house. Many people do this and they do it automatically to the point where they don't even remember doing it.

The second category are habits that we need to work at because they're good for us, like exercising, or going to bed at a certain time to get enough sleep. These are the habits you want to work on to help you go farther in life, or to achieve certain goals like making a team, learning a new skill, or even getting a scholarship. (These are the habits you'll learn about in this chapter.)

The third and final category are habits that are bad for us, like smoking, overeating, overspending, procrastinating. Some habits are so bad for people, they end up living on the streets as a result of them, unable to hold down a job or be healthy. While you'd think habits like this would be easy to break–who wants to live in a tent? --unfortunately, without the motivation and the knowledge to break old habits and create new ones, this can be hard to do. But why does this happen? Why can't people just stop the bad routines and start the great habits without any problems?

Science has the answer.

Psychology and Our Habits

Researchers have determined that there's a part of the brain called the *basal ganglia* which plays a role in making new habits and maintaining the ones we already have. They found this while trying to learn why people with major brain injuries still performed certain actions or were able to remember specific things like how to find their way home even if they weren't able to recall where they lived. As long as the basal ganglia is uninjured, we will maintain certain ingrained habits even when we no longer need or benefit from them (Soots 2015).

Another thing researchers have learned is that over 40% of what we do every day is not due to conscious decisions but by rituals we've already established. This means that we can change parts of our lives by getting rid of old ways and creating new ones–possibly better ones–instead.

The question then becomes–how?

The Anatomy of Habit

Researchers at the Massachusetts Institute of Technology (MIT) did a study where they found that habits are formed of three neurological parts. They called this "the habit loop"(Learning Center n.d.):

1-Cue

Cue is considered the trigger of habit; it tells your brain to go into automatic mode and starts the habitual behavior.

2-Routine

This is the behavior part of the habit and the resulting actions.

3- Reward

This is the part of the "habit loop" that determines whether or not a habit is worth developing and remembering. Rewards can be either immediate or delayed; habits are easier to form if the reward is immediate.

Once you understand how habits form, you can easily figure out how to build new ones and break old ones. For example, let's say that every day after school you pass by a McD's and–because you're hungry–you stop in and grab a large fry. (Routine) Once in a while, this would be fine, but it's become a habit. In fact, as the final bell rings (Cue), your stomach starts to growl and your mouth begins to water as your body prepares to consume those hot, salty, greasy fries (Reward). Even on days you don't have school, right around the time (Cue) you'd be passing that McDonald's, your body is saying, "Where are my fries?" (Routine)

But we learned in the previous chapter that nutrition is important; the salt and saturated fat content of these fries can make you sluggish, make you bloated, and—in fact—make you sick. Except—you're hungry! You crave them!

How can you break this habit? By disrupting the loop. Sure, you could just say no to stopping into the restaurant and walk right by the door without getting your fries. But your body is still going to growl and complain. You might get *hangry*, and end up stopping at a different restaurant and creating a new (bad) habit by substituting a different type of bad-for-you food.

In this case, the best thing to do would be to prepare a healthy substitute ahead of time. Something simple and easy to carry, maybe a piece (or pieces) of fresh fruit, or a few low-fat cheese sticks, or some trail mix made with nuts, seeds, and dried fruit...something nutritious to fill that hole in your belly. Keep in mind, your body will complain for a few days—it's been conditioned to accept that salty, greasy snack. (And, let's face it, fries *are* delicious!) But it will adjust, and in no time at all, it will be craving that new snack when the final bell rings to go home.

More Tips to Break Old Habits and Make New Ones

1- Start with small adjustments.

Some habits are harder to break than the example I used above. In some cases, you're going to have to really work at it, especially if you want to create a new habit. Experts suggest that you work on developing a new habit a little at a time and be patient. As I mentioned in chapter six, it takes a person (on average) at least 21 days to develop a new habit; if you expect to make a big change immediately and make it become a habit, you will probably fail.

2-Be positive.

Even though I just said something kind of negative about creating a new habit, you should still be positive. Being positive doesn't mean ignoring bad things or instances, but it *does* mean reacting to things positively, with a good attitude. So if you do decide to make a big change in one major move, accept the fact that you might fail and acknowledge that, but don't go in expecting and anticipating that you are definitely going to fail.

3-Commit to your change.

Accept the fact that you're going to meet obstacles and experience problems by meeting these challenges with a positive attitude. Stay committed to your new habit and your odds of success will greatly increase.

4-Take time to think about what's holding you back.

Sometimes it's not the good habit that is hard to adopt. Instead, it's all the things that come along with it that make it difficult to achieve. Finding the ideal answer to these issues is simpler after you identified the factors holding you back.

5-Plan with failure in mind.

Even if you're positive and have a good attitude about your new habit, you might fail at it. Sometimes this failure makes you give up on your attempt, but if you plan for how to respond to this failure, you can get back on track. It's kind of like the old saying, "If at first you don't succeed, try and try again."

The thing is, it's normal to be unsuccessful at first. But the people who eventually create new habits are the ones who have a plan to deal with their failure and make the habit happen anyway.

6-Get support from friends and family.

Let your family and friends know about your desire to create a new habit and they can help you.

7-Celebrate your small wins.

We discussed this in chapter four when I said that smaller, short-term, and attainable goals are easier to achieve. Same thing about new habits. When you succeed, you are rewarded, which motivates you to keep going and achieve even more.

8-Work on your environment.

If you don't change your environment to set yourself up for success, it will be more difficult to eliminate bad habits and create new ones. So if there is anything you can change, do it! An example of this would be wanting to cut down on the processed sugar in your diet but only having a kitchen full of cakes, cookies, and ice cream to eat. Obviously, you need to set up your environment by getting rid of the sugary foods and replacing them with healthy, non-processed-sugar-filled things.

9-Focus on building a routine to create a new habit and eliminate an old one.

In order to make a new habit, you need to do it daily and regularly to make it part of your routine.

10-Have clarity.

Make sure you know why you're making this change in your habits. If you have a clear and strong reason for it, and know the importance of your new habit in your life, you are more likely to have success.

11-Replace self-judgment with self-compassion.

This was mentioned in chapter six when I wrote you should talk to yourself as you'd talk to a friend. When you are trying to create a new habit—and slip—you need to motivate yourself with a positive "you can do this" and not discourage yourself by telling yourself that you can't. The reason for this is because when you self-judge, you run the risk of taking on feelings of blame and guilt.

Be compassionate toward yourself. Give yourself empathy. And be positive!

12-Be patient with yourself.

Forming a new habit takes time; it's not going to happen immediately. You need to let it sink in and become a part of your neurological map. Be patient with yourself, and keep on working on it.

13-Focus on one habit at a time.

When you decide on some new habits to create, it's easy to think you can do it all at once; you're enthused and you're sure you're going to be successful. Then it starts to get difficult. And then you quit because you've done too much, too soon.

By focusing on one change at a time, you're going to be more successful. Work on prioritizing the habits by order of importance and then tackle them one at a time to ensure your success.

14-Create a habit journal.

Using a journal to track your success when you start a new habit will motivate you to continue working. At the same time, using a journal to record your failures can help you understand your mistakes so that you can try again–this time with success (Week Plan 2020).

Some important habits for you to develop as an athlete

Now that you know some ways to make habits easier to form, let's discuss some specific habits you can work on to improve your success as an athlete (In Your Home Therapy 2020).

- **A dynamic warm-up:** Create a habit of a vigorous workout using push-ups, jumping jacks, and other exercises designed to get your heart pumping and your muscles ready for action.
- **Rest and recovery:** Make resting and allowing your body to recover part of your training program. Drink water, eat properly, and get

enough rest (doctors recommend six to eight hours of sleep a night for good health).

- **Listening to your body:** Make it a habit to listen to your body; if you feel pain, stop and be sure it's not a serious injury. If you're hungry, eat. If you need to sleep–sleep! Your body knows what it needs; all you have to do is listen.

- **Focusing on quality instead of quantity:** Use proper form for your skills training; doing a few movements perfectly is better than many reps of your skills using bad form or sloppiness (which will create bad habits and a lack of success).

- **Making a habit of hydration:** Start your day with at least 6 oz. of water, and drink frequently throughout the day. Drink more if you're active or if the weather is warm.

- **Building your core strength:** Make core exercises a part of your workout routine; try to do them two to three days a week. Core strength helps to support your back and all of your torso and makes it easier to move.

USING VISUALIZATION TO CHANGE YOUR HABITS

You can use visualization for many things, even changing your habits. Say, for example, you realize you have a habit of being indecisive during a play. You just get in your own head and, instead of reacting as you would during practice, you freeze. In fact, you expect to freeze up; you lose all confidence in your abilities.

Remember back in chapter one when we discussed practicing your practice mindset? This brings us right back to that section. Use visualization to change this habit of overthinking and just play like you're practicing.

1- Change your emotions:

The most important part of eliminating a bad habit is the desire to do it. Once you're committed, there's nothing you can't do! One way to approach this is by changing your emotions (visually) about a situation. Like, indecisiveness during a play.

When you visualize yourself freezing up, not sure how to proceed, and losing your opportunity, how does that make you feel? Pretty bad, I'm sure. Incompetent, lame, pathetic…that's how I'd feel, anyway. Find and identify your feelings at that moment. Then, begin to imagine calm flowing through you instead. Confidence. Determination. Let these positive feelings soak in and replace the negative feelings that often occur during the moments of indecision.

2-Visualize and create a new outcome for the scenario:

As we've discussed, the key to visualization is repetition and practice. So using that scenario above, create a new outcome by not only replacing the negative emotions that make you indecisive, but by completely envisioning yourself without that habit at all.

Use all the means and methods of visualization we've discussed: finding your space and place, clearing your mind and focusing, using all your senses, and imagining yourself at that place where you'd ordinarily freeze up—then move past it by visualizing yourself reacting instinctively and making the play perfectly. And then repeat this visualization. Practice makes perfect, as the saying goes—so practice your visualization and *get* perfect! You'll find that with repetition, your visualization will become stronger, more clear, and more vibrant. When you do that, it will become your new habit (Selfgrowth n.d.).

Making Visualization into a Habit

As meta as it sounds, you can create a habit of visualization (but *not* by visualizing yourself visualizing as a habit…gosh, that's confusing.) Let me try to be more clear.

As stated repeatedly (because it can't be said enough), the only way to make visualization work is by practicing visualizing. So you need to create a habit of visualization by:

- Visualizing every day. As we've discussed throughout this book, you can't just visualize one time and expect things to change. You need to be consistent and persistent. Don't give up. It's going to take work. But, as with anything you work on, it will show positive results.

Use visualization tools and techniques, like:

- Using an anchor (remember the index-finger to thumb trick discussed in chapter six?)
- Creating a vision board
- Writing down your goals
- Mentally practicing along with your actual practice
- Visualizing your life after you've reached your goals
- Picturing everything you need to in great detail
- Setting mini-goals for yourself to achieve and celebrate

- Zoning out and daydreaming

(O'Neal 2021)

EXERCISE #8: MASTERING YOUR HABITS

Take stock of your habits. You can focus only on habits that you can associate with your sporting activities or the entire range of habits that you have. List your habits according to the following:

- Good habits that you already have but you think could use some enhancement.
- Bad habits you know you have and are keen on changing or eliminating completely.
- Great habits (especially related to your sports activities and goals) that you currently don't have, like those discussed in a previous section.

Use your knowledge of how to manipulate the Habit Loop to enhance one habit in your list at a time. Remember, the habit loop consists of the cue, the routine, and the reward; you need to change one of these things (or all of them, depending on what the habit is) in order to eliminate an old habit and create a new one.

FINAL WORDS

"Gooooooooooal! Gooooooooooooaaaaaallll!"

— *FAMOUS SOCCER ANNOUNCER,*
ANDRES CANTOR

I think Andres puts it best here. We kicked it over the line and we scored. Gooooal!

Through the course of this book, we've discussed how you can train your brain to be clutch by understanding and learning to overcome your pregame anxiety by using visualization, goal setting, and confidence building. We've discussed good nutrition for athletes to prepare your body for your sport, and we've talked about creating good habits to make you be the clutch player you want to become.

Ultimately, you've learned that there is an undeniable connection between the mind and athletic performance, not only in your own life but in the lives and careers of professional athletes. In all areas of sports, the elite, clutch athletes know the value of visualization and use it routinely to become the top players in their games.

They use visualization to overcome pregame anxiety, or to harness the energy of their nerves to strengthen their performance and master their mental state and the emotions that result from it. In many cases, they also use visualization to enhance every aspect of their performance and employ it to set goals and increase their focus.

It's important to point out that setting goals in sports is like setting goals in anything else; learning to set goals and work correctly to achieve them through visualization provides you with the highest possibility of bringing your goals to fruition. Visualization is a powerful tool that can remap the neural paths in your brain to bring you greater confidence and even improve your skills. Used in conjunction with practicing your techniques, and used consistently and daily, it will bring you to a higher level of sports performance.

Keep your eyes on your goals...

All you need to do is think of Michael Jordan, considered to be one of the greatest NBA players of all time. You may have heard that Jordan was cut from his varsity basketball team during his sophomore year, but did you know he responded by learning to use visualization? (Connors 2016)

With a combination of visualization and an increase in physical practice to improve his ball handling, his quickness, and his jump shot, Jordan eventually earned a scholarship to the University of North Carolina. There, he won a national championship and–in his final season–was named National Player of the Year.

About this, Jordan said, "I visualized where I wanted to be, what kind of player I wanted to become. I knew exactly where I wanted to go, and I focused on getting there." He used visualization to envision himself making game-winning shots before he even set foot on the court. His imagination lifted his confidence, fueled his drive, and gave him the belief in himself that he needed to become the elite athlete we all now recognize him to be.

...and don't forget the importance of good nutrition!

It's important to point out that no matter how much natural talent you possess, or how well you visualize, or how much you practice to perfect your skills. Your vision, talent, or skill can only carry your body so far. There are no shortcuts when it comes to good nutrition. Especially, when it comes to hydration!

In 2014, tennis player Andy Murray discovered the truth of this when he was almost overwhelmed by head-to-toe cramping during the U.S. Open. In spite of this, he went on to win his match against opponent Robin Haase. Murray had trained in Miami, in more heat and humidity than occurred that day on the court; only his focus and skills–and his ability to be clutch– pushed him to win regardless of the crippling cramps. Still, Murray was left to muse if the problem came from his nutrition (Columbia Daily Tribune n.d.).

The reality is that as a young athlete– or an athlete at any level of their game– proper nutrition is key for success; make it a habit to fuel your body properly and well.

Above all, don't let your failures stop you from succeeding.

Mental training is just as important as physical training and talent when it comes to athletic performance. The good news is that the mind can be sharpened and programmed to lead you to success in any field of sports.

Michael Jordan is quoted as saying, *"I've missed more than 9000 shots in my career. I've lost almost 300 games. 26 times, I've been trusted to take the game winning shot and missed. I've failed over and over and over again in my life. And that is why I succeed* (Connors 2016)."

I love this quote because it comes from an athlete who was at the top of his game when he said it, and he wasn't bragging about how great he was but sharing his motivation to be the best and even better. It reminds all of us that through bad can come good, and especially that you don't have to let your failures define you. Instead, you can use them as fuel for your success.

I like to remind anyone I work with that every miss is an opportunity to learn and to grow. And, as Adam Sandler's wife tells him in the movie, *Hustle*, it's never about the last play but on the next one. As an athlete, you need to live in the present and prepare for the future but never get stuck in the past. Jordan shows us this by admitting that, yes, he's had some failures, but he's moved past them to succeed.

Using the tools and examples in this book, you not only can think about being clutch–clutch is what you can be.

Putting the ideas and techniques I've shown you into practice and into play will get you there, "just like Mike" (Schultz et al. 2002). The best part is—you can start visualizing yourself being clutch right now.

A Final (final) Word

If you've found this book helpful, please tell your team-mates, coaches, teachers, and friends about it. I'm passionate about bringing the message and technique of visualization for success in sports—and other parts of life—to everyone. Please let me know how I've helped you be clutch **by writing a review** and letting everyone know—it will bring this to so many more athletes and people who can benefit from visualization.

Thank you!

REFERENCES

Adams, AJ. "Seeing Is Believing: The Power of Visualization." Psychology Today. December 3, 2009.https://www.psychologyto day.com/us/blog/flourish/200912/seeing-is-believing-the-power-visualization.

Alaia, Michael, MD.; "Sports Nutrition - OrthoInfo - AAOS." 2014. Aaos.org. 2014. August 2019. https://orthoinfo.aaos.org/en/stay ing-healthy/sports-nutrition/.

Alexander Kuhn, M. "How to Teach Youth Athletes to Set Goals." Stack. November 19, 2020. https://www.stack.com/a/teach-athletes-goal-setting/

Anderson, Ty. "Patriots QB Tom Brady Still Gets Nervous before Big Games." 2019. 98.5 the Sports Hub - Boston's Home for Sports. January 19, 2019. https://985thesportshub.com/2019/01/19/patri ots-qb-tom-brady-still-gets-nervous-before-big-games/.

ATHLETE IQ. "Coping with Pregame Anxiety: Part 1." March 15, 2020. https://athleteiq.com.au/coping-with-pregame-anxiety-part-1/

Brooks, Elise. "Goals and Visualization" Leveraged Writings. March 12, 2021. https://leveragedwritings.com/setting-goals-and-visualiza tion/.

Central Orthopedic Group. "6 Best Foods for Sports Injury Recovery." October 31, 2018. https://centralorthopedicgroup.com/6-best-foods-eat-recovering-sports-injuries/.

Cohn, Patrick, Dr.; "Mental Training Success Stories | Peak Perfor-mance Sports." September 7, 2012. https://www.peaksports.com/sports-psychology-case-studies/.

Columbia Daily Tribune. "Murray Grits through Cramps to Win at U.S. Open." (n.d.) Accessed July 25, 2022. https://www.columbiatri bune.com/story/news/2014/08/26/murray-grits-through-cramps-to/21729153007/.

Connors, Christopher D. "The Formula That Leads to Wild Success-Part 1: Michael Jordan." Medium. Mission.org. June 16, 2016. https://medium.com/the-mission/the-formula-that-leads-to-wild-success-part-1-michael-jordan-8d3fe552592.

Doc Bear. "How to Break Down Game Film: A Beginner's Guide." n.d. Denver Broncos. Dec 11, 2015. https://247sports.com/nfl/denver-broncos/Article/How-To-Break-Down-Game-Film-A-Beginners-Guide-75025141/.

Elliott, Dave, Remco Polman, and Julie Taylor. "The Effects of Relaxing Music for Anxiety Control on Competitive Sport Anxiety." *European Journal of Sport Science* 14 (sup1): S296–301. 2012. https://doi.org/10.1080/17461391.2012.693952.

ESPN Internet Ventures. (2014, August 25). *Novak Djokovic rolls at US open*. ESPN. Retrieved July 22, 2022, from https://www.espn.com/tennis/usopen14/story/_/id/11408284/2014-us-open-andy-murray-grits-cramps-win-first-round

Fan, Ryan. 2019. "How Can We Be More Clutch?" The Startup. June 1, 2019. https://medium.com/swlh/how-can-we-be-more-clutch-6841f605f7ae.

Ferber, Taylor. "These Professional Athletes' Pre-Performance Rituals Will Inspire You to Get Moving." Bustle. July 19, 2017. https://www.bustle.com/p/these-professional-athletes-pre-performance-rituals-will-inspire-you-to-get-moving-71137.

Gloveworx. "What You Need to Know about Competitive State Anxiety." February 15, 2018. https://www.gloveworx.com/blog/what-you-need-know-about-competitive-state-anxiety/.

"Gregg Popovich." Wikipedia. June 25, 2022. https://en.wikipedia.org/wiki/Gregg_Popovich.

Hamilton, Andrew. "Sports Psychology: Self-Confidence in Sport – Make Your Ego Work for You!" Sports Performance Bulletin. February 17, 2017. https://www.sportsperformancebulletin.com/endurance-psychology/coping-with-emotions/sports-psychology-self-confidence-sport-make-ego-work/.

Hamilton, David. "Real vs Imaginary in the Brain and Body." 2019.

David R Hamilton PHD. February 19, 2019. https://drdavidhamil ton.com/real-vs-imaginary-in-the-brain-and-body/.

Harmer, Katherine R. D. N. (2020, September 16). *Best supplements for teenage athletes*. Fueling Teens -Nutrition and Wellness for Teens. Retrieved July 30, 2022, from https://www.fuelingteens.com/best-supplements/

Harris, Thomas R. "25+ SMART Goals Examples for Life and Work (Both Quick and Detailed Examples) - the Exceptional Skills." March 4, 2019. https://www.theexceptionalskills.com/smart-goals-examples/.

Hims. (n.d.) "Visualization Techniques and Exercises for Anxiety." Accessed July 8, 2022. https://www.forhims.com/blog/visualiza tion-techniques.

History.com. (n.d.) "U.S. Hockey Team Makes Miracle on Ice." Accessed June 25, 2022. https://www.history.com/this-day-in-history/u-s-hockey-team-makes-miracle-on-ice

Hutchison, Moira. "5 Ways to Visualize Yourself as Confident · the Wellness Universe Blog." The Wellness Universe Blog. August 18, 2018. https://blog.thewellnessuniverse.com/5-ways-visualize-your self-confident/.

In Your Home Therapy. "7 Healthy Habits for All Athletes." October 26, 2020. https://www.inyourhometherapy.com/our-blog/7-healthy-habits-for-all-athletes/.

"Information from Your Patient Aligned Care Team Visualiza-tion/Guided Imagery." Accessed July 10, 2022. https://www.mirecc. va.gov/cih-visn2/Documents/Patient_Education_Handouts/ Visualization_Guided_Image

Jenkins, Rhiannon. What Is Sports Psychology and Why Is It Important for Athletes? Jenkins Soft Tissue Therapy. February 23, 2020. https://jenkinstherapy.com/blog/what-is-sports-psychology-and-why-is-it-important-for-athletes/

Kuloor, Haridas, and Ashok Kumar. "Self-Confidence and Sports." Accessed December 5, 2021. https://doi.org/10.25215/0804.001.

Kuhn, M. A. *How to teach youth athletes to set goals*. stack. 2021,

November 12. Retrieved July 30, 2022, from https://www.stack.com/a/teach-athletes-goal-setting/

LaBorde, Susan. "Why Visualization Works - and the Famous Athletes Who've Used It." Make a Vision Board. (Modified May 14, 2019) Accessed June 20, 2022. https://makeavisionboard.com/why-visualization-works/.

Leal, Darla. "An Overview of Sports Nutrition." Verywell Fit. Verywellfit. February 5, 2018. https://www.verywellfit.com/fitness-sports-nutrition 1167143

Learning Center. "Changing Habits - Learning Center." University of North Carolina. (n.d.) Accessed June 20, 2022. https://learningcenter.unc.edu/tips-and-tools/changing-habits/.

Losilla, Nacho. "The Story of Ray Allen's Last-Second Three, the Most Clutch Shot in NBA History." n.d. Www.sportingnews.com. June 18, 2020. https://www.sportingnews.com/ca/nba/news/the-story-of-ray-allens-last-second-three-the-clutchest-shot-in-nba-history/17zdyy370bzjw107y8lq1ajacn.

Louw, Bennie. "Why Do Athletes Perform Better in Practice than in Competition!?" n.d. SportMindCoach. (n.d.) Accessed June 27, 2022. https://sportmindcoach.co.za/why-do-athletes-perform-better-in-practice-than-in-competition/.

Mark. *7 reasons you play better in practice than performance.* Play In The Zone. March 25, 2019. Retrieved July 30, 2022, from https://playinthezone.com/play-better-practice-performance/

McDermott, J. *Why So Many Athletes Have Such Terrible Diets.* Mel. 2017. Retrieved July 2022, from https://melmagazine.com/en-us/story/why-so-many-athletes-have-such-terrible-diets

Mental training success stories: Peak performance sports. Peak Performance Sports | Sports Psychology Coaching for Athletes. Parents, Coaches. (2018, August 14). Retrieved July 30, 2022, from https://www.peaksports.com/sports-psychology-case-studies/

Mind Tools. Smart Goals: How to make your goals achievable. (n.d.) https://www.mindtools.com/pages/article/smart-goals.htm

Moore, Catherine. "11+ Mindset Activities and Tests Designed to

Nurture Growth." 2019. PositivePsychology.com. December 10, 2019. https://positivepsychology.com/mindset-activities-tests/.

O'Neal, R. *How to make visualization a habit? (correct answer)*. Blog about habits and tips. November 25, 2021. Retrieved July 30, 2022, from https://www.toridawnselden.com/all-about-habits/how-to-make-visualization-a-habit-correct-answer.html

Otten, Mark. "The Psychology of the Clutch Athlete." The Conversation. October 24, 2017. https://theconversation.com/the-psychology-of-the-clutch-athlete-85956.

Pakarinen, Risto. "1980 Soviet Union Squad Was History's Greatest International Hockey Team." ABC News. September 15, 2016. https://abcnews.go.com/Sports/1980-soviet-union-squad-historys-greatest-international-hockey/story?id=42117760

Pichee, Aimee. "Cheesecake Factory Dinged as Unhealthiest U.S. Eatery." n.d. Www.cbsnews.com. July 31, 2014. https://www.cbsnews.com/news/cheesecake-factory-dinged-as-unhealthiest-u-s-eatery/.

Predoiu, R. *Visualisation techniques in sport - the mental road map for success*. Researchgate.Net. September 2020. Retrieved July 2022, from https://www.researchgate.net/publication/344587632_Visualisation_techniques_in_sport_-_the_mental_road_map_for_success

Randolph, Keith. "Sports Visualizations." Llewellyn.com. May 15, 2002. Accessed July 7, 2022. https://www.llewellyn.com/encyclopedia/article/244.

Raypole, Crystal. "How to Hack Your Hormones for a Better Mood." Healthline. Healthline Media. September 30, 2019. https://www.healthline.com/health/happy-hormone.

Schleien, Danny. 2021. "What Tom Brady Can Teach You about Confidence." Mind Cafe. January 29, 2021. https://medium.com/mind-cafe/what-tom-brady-can-teach-you-about-confidence-75fb9a467675.

Schultz, John, Michael Elliot, Michael Elliot, Jordan Moffet, Shad Moss, Jonathan Lipnicki, Morris Chestnut, and Brenda Song. 2002.

"Like Mike." IMDb. July 3, 2002. https://www.imdb.com/title/tt0308506/.

Scott, S.J. "Goal Setting Activities of Olympic Athletes (and What They Can Teach the Rest of Us)." Develop Good Habits. August 13, 2013. https://www.developgoodhabits.com/goal-setting-activities/.

Selfgrowth.com. "Use Visualization to Change Your Habits." Www.selfgrowth.com. (n.d.) Accessed July 22, 2022. :https //www.selfgrowth.com/articles/use-visualization-to-change-your-habits.

Shintani. *What You Should Know if You Play Better in Practice than in Games*. Mind Body Sports. 2021. Retrieved 2022, from https://www.mind-designsports.org/blogs/what-you-should-know-if-you-play-better-in-practice-vs-games

Sigl, Craig. "How to Do Visualization Effectively for Sports." 2014. Mental Toughness Trainer. (n.d.) Accessed June 20, 2022. https://www.mentaltoughnesstrainer.com/visualization-techniques-for-sports/.

Simpson, Maclin. "Make Mental Imagery Your Weapon of Confidence." Www.floswimming.com. May 22, 2017. https://www.floswimming.com/articles/5065673-make-mental-imagery-your-weapon-of-confidence.

Soots, Lynn. "What Are Habits? - the Positive Psychology People." The Positive Psychology People. August 30, 2015. https://www.thepositivepsychologypeople.com/habits-to-happiness/.

Sports Psychology History. (n.d.) Accessed July 15, 2022. http://psychology.iresearchnet.com/sports-psychology/sports-psychology-history/

Taylor, J. *Sport imagery: Athletes' most powerful mental tool*. Psychology Today. November 6, 2012. Retrieved July 30, 2022, from https://www.psychologytoday.com/us/blog/the-power-prime/201211/sport-imagery-athletes-most-powerful-mental-tool

Thorp, T. *How to use meditation to visualize your goals*. Chopra. 2021, June 28. Retrieved July 30, 2022, from https://chopra.com/articles/how-to-use-meditation-to-visualize-your-goals

US Hockey Hall of Fame. *The 1980 U.S. Olympic Hockey Team*. Retrieved

July 2022, from https://www.ushockeyhalloffame.com/page/show/831562-the-1980-u-s-olympic-team

Week Plan. "15 Key Tips to Develop Good Habits." Week Plan. January 1, 2020. https://weekplan.net/tips-to-develop-good-habits.

Weiland, Bianca, "5 Benefits of Visualization for Everyday Runners and Athletes." ActivAcuity. January 14, 2016. https://www.activacuity.com/2016/01/5-benefits-of-visualization-for-everyday-runners-and-athletes/.

Williams, Lauren. "10 Athletes Who Meditate." n.d. The Yogi Press. November 2, 2018. https://www.yogi.press/home/10-athletes-who-meditate.

Yeager, S. *Pregame rituals of the pros*. ESPN.Com. August 15, 2011. https://www.espn.com/espnw/training/story/_/id/6857252/pregame-rituals-pros

Zagar, Jeremiah, Taylor Materne, Will Fetters, Adam Sandler, Queen Latifah, and Juancho Hernangomez. 2022. "Hustle." IMDb. June 8, 2022. https://www.imdb.com/title/tt8009428/.

Made in the USA
Las Vegas, NV
12 February 2024